THE PUPIL
AS SCIENTIST?

THE PUPIL AS SCIENTIST?

Rosalind Driver
University of Leeds

OPEN UNIVERSITY PRESS

Milton Keynes · Philadelphia

Open University Press
Celtic Court
22 Ballmoor
Buckingham
MK18 1XW
and
1900 Frost Road, Suite 101
Bristol, PA 19007, USA

First published 1983

Reprinted 1985, 1986, 1988, 1991, 1993

British Library Cataloguing in Publication Data

Driver, Rosalind
  The pupil as scientist?
  1. Science—Study and teaching
  I. Title
  507'.1   LB1585

ISBN 0 335 10178 X

Printed in Great Britain by St Edmundsbury Press Limited,
Bury St Edmunds, Suffolk.

CONTENTS

PREFACE

Discovery methods in science teaching put pupils in the role of investigator, giving them opportunities to perform experiments and test ideas for themselves. What actually happens in classrooms when this approach is used? Although, of course, pupils' ideas are less sophisticated than those of practising scientists, some interesting parallels can be drawn. The work of Thomas Kuhn indicates that, once a scientific theory or paradigm becomes established, scientists as a community are slow to change their thinking. Pupils, like scientists, view the world through the spectacles of their own preconceptions, and many have difficulty in making the journey from their own intuitions to the ideas presented in science lessons.

This book is an attempt to describe events along the path of the pupil as scientist. Its intention is to be descriptive rather than prescriptive. It contains many examples of pupils' dialogue and written work. Most of the examples were collected while making a study over a 4-month period of a science class at the University of Illinois Curriculum Laboratory. As the excerpts indicate, the teacher encouraged the class to investigate phenomena and to make their own inferences. In order to indicate in some detail the development in pupils' thinking, a small group of pupils was selected for detailed study.

Further examples from other science lessons have also been used. Most of these are examples of pupils' work from classes I have observed or taught myself.

The first chapter of the book makes the case that pupils do come to science lessons with already formulated ideas, or alternative frameworks, and that these may be at variance with the theories the teacher may wish to develop. The examples in this chapter also illustrate the fallacy of the simple inductive method in science teaching.

In later chapters I give further examples of common alternative frameworks, and how these affect pupils' observations and the sense they make of them.

Currently, research on children's thinking in science is focused on the development of children's logical abilities. A further chapter indicates, with examples, the limitations of this position in understanding children's thinking, and suggests that more attention needs to be paid to the development of specific ideas and concepts as opposed to generalized thinking skills.

Inevitably, the book raises questions about classroom practice. Here I recognize the danger of being prescriptive and recommending simplistic solutions to complex problems. However, implications for secondary science courses are raised and general suggestions for classroom practice are made in the last chapter.

A paper outlining a method for representing children's frameworks in science, with particular reference to ideas in dynamics, is included in the Appendix.

ACKNOWLEDGEMENTS

This book owes much to the friendly cooperation and patience of five pupils, Jane, Richard, Carl, Tim and Cathy. I would like to express my thanks to them and to their teacher, Larry Guthrie, for allowing me to be present during their lessons.

I am also grateful to Pat Butcher for her patience and care in the preparation of the manuscript.

Examples of classroom activities described on pages 6, 7, 44 and 47 were first published in the *European Journal for Science Education* and are used with permission of the publishers, Taylor & Francis Ltd.

1

THE FALLACY OF INDUCTION
IN SCIENCE TEACHING

Science is not just a collection of laws, a catalogue of facts,
it is a creation of the human mind with its freely invented
ideas and concepts. Physical theories try to form a picture
of reality and to establish its connections with the wide
world of sense impressions.

A. Einstein and L. Infield,
The Evolution of Physics, (1938).

In our everyday life as adults we operate with a very complex
set of beliefs and expectations about events. An egg rolls
across the counter top in the kitchen and we know where to
make a grasp for it before it falls over the edge and smashes
to the floor. The fact that so many of us can drive around on
our roads without more accidents occurring is possible because
of the sets of expectations we have developed enabling us to
predict the speed and movement of other vehicles on the
road and the probable behaviour of pedestrians. Such sets of
expectations mean we can live our daily lives without being
constantly in a state of disorientation and shock. Similarly,
children construct sets of expectations or beliefs about a
range of natural phenomena in their efforts to make sense of
everyday experiences.

A 10-year-old switched off the radio, noticed with surprise that it took over a second for the sound to fade away
and commented: 'What a long length of electric wire there
must be in that radio when you think how fast electricity
travels.' Without any formal instruction, this child had
already developed certain ideas about electricity, notably
that it travels down wires, and that it travels very fast.

From the very earliest days in its life, a child develops beliefs about the things that happen in its surroundings. The baby lets go of a rattle and it falls to the ground; it does it again and the pattern repeats itself. It pushes a ball and it goes on rolling across the floor. In this way, sets of expectations are established which enable the child to begin to make predictions. Initially, these are isolated and independent of one another. However, as the child grows older, all its experiences of pushing, pulling, lifting, throwing, feeling and seeing things stimulate the development of more generalized sets of expectations and the ability to make predictions about a progressively wider range of experiences. By the time the child receives formal teaching in science it has already constructed a set of beliefs about a range of natural phenomena. In some cases, these beliefs or intuitions are strongly held and may differ from the accepted theories which science teaching aims to communicate.

One of the features of the science teaching schemes which have been developed over the last 20 or 30 years is a rejection of science as a catalogue of facts. Instead, teaching schemes have been produced which present science as a coherent system of ideas. Focus is on the integrating concepts or big ideas such as atomic theory in chemistry or kinetic theory in physics. Apart from doing justice to the nature of scientific theory itself, one of the important arguments for such an approach suggested by Bruner[1] is that it helps pupils to apply ideas to new situations if the connections between those ideas are made explicit in teaching. Put in psychologists' jargon, it encourages 'transfer'.

One of the problems with this argument is that the connections that are apparent to a scientist may be far from obvious to a pupil. It is, after all, the coherence as perceived by the pupil that matters in learning. In developing science teaching material little attention has yet been paid to the ideas which children themselves bring to the learning task, yet these may have a significant influence on what children can and do learn from their science lessons. Over a decade ago, the psychologist David Ausubel commented on the importance of considering what he called children's preconceptions, suggesting that they are 'amazingly tenacious and resistant to extinction . . .' and that '. . . unlearning of preconceptions might well prove to be the most determinative single factor in the acquisition and retention of subject matter knowledge'.[2]

This perspective on learning suggests that it is as important in teaching and curriculum development to consider and understand children's own ideas as it is to give a clear presentation of the conventional scientific theories. After all, if a visitor phones you up explaining he has got lost on the way to your home, your first reaction would probably be to ask 'Where are you now?' You cannot start to give sensible directions without knowing where your visitor is starting from. Similarly, in teaching science it is important in designing teaching programmes to take into account both children's own ideas and those of the scientific community.

By the time children are taught science in school, their expectations or beliefs about natural phenomena may be well developed. In some cases these intuitions are in keeping with the ideas pupils will meet in their science lessons. They may be poorly articulated but they provide a base on which formal learning can build. However, in other cases the accepted theory may be counter-intuitive with pupils' own beliefs and expectations differing in significant ways from those to be taught. Such beliefs I shall refer to as 'alternative frameworks'. This book explores aspects of the relationship between pupils' alternative frameworks and science teaching: how they affect pupils' interpretations of the practical experiences given in science lessons and influence the observations made.

Another characteristic of the science curriculum development of the last few decades has been an emphasis on the heuristic method. This was prompted by the admirable concern to allow children to experience something of the excitement of science—'to be a scientist for a day'.[3] We are now recognizing the pitfalls of putting this approach into practice in classrooms and laboratories. Secondary school pupils are quick to recognize the rules of the game when they ask 'Is this what was supposed to happen?' or 'Have I got the right answer?'[4,5] The intellectual dishonesty of the approach derives from expecting two outcomes from pupils' laboratory activities which are possibly incompatible. On the one hand pupils are expected to explore a phenomenon for themselves, collect data and make inferences based on it; on the other hand this process is intended to lead to the currently accepted scientific law or principle.

Some insight into this problem can be gained by considering different views of the nature of science. The most simplistic view of the scientific enterprise is, perhaps, the empiricist's view, which holds that all knowledge is based on observation. Scientific laws are reached by a process of induction from the 'facts' of sense data. Taking this view of science, observations are objective and facts immutable. Also, such a position asserts that science will produce a steady growth in knowledge: like some international game of 'pass the parcel', the truth about the natural world will be unwrapped and gradually more will be revealed.

This inductivist position was criticized when it was first suggested by Bacon nearly 400 years ago, yet it has reasserted itself early in this century in the heuristic movement and later in some of the more naive interpretations of the discovery method adopted by the Nuffield science schemes.

For a long time philosophers of science and scientists themselves have recognized the limitations of the inductivist position and have acknowledged the important role that imagination plays in the construction of scientific theories. In this alternative constructivist or hypothetico-deductive view, theories are not related by induction to sense data, but are constructions of the human mind whose link with the world of experience comes through the processes by which they are tested and evaluated.

Currently there are different views about the criteria for acceptance or rejection of scientific theories.[6] The philosopher Popper asserts that, in addition to the individual's mental world, there exists a world of objective knowledge[7] which has properties which can be assessed by logical principles without regard to the person or group of people who generated that knowledge. Others subscribe to a more subjective position. Polanyi,[8] for example, in his writings, indicates the importance of the commitment of an individual to a theory, a commitment which may be influenced by factors other than logic, with aesthetic criteria playing an important part. Science as a cooperative exercise as opposed to an individual venture is emphasized in the writings of Kuhn[9] and Lakatos[10]. Viewed from a sociological perspective, such writers suggest that the criterion for acceptance of a scientific theory is that it is scrutinized and approved by the community of scientists.

Although there are these differences of view on the objectivity of scientific knowledge and the criteria for assessing theories, there is general agreement on two matters of importance to school science. The first is the recognition of pluralism in scientific theories. Following from this is acceptance of the revolutionary nature of science; that progress in scientific knowledge comes about through major changes in scientists' theories (or paradigms). This gives science educators the task of 'teaching consensus without turning it into an orthodoxy.'[11] The second point of agreement is about the nature of observations: these are no longer seen as objective but influenced by the theoretical perspective of the observer.[12] As Popper said, '. . . we are prisoners caught in the framework of our theories'.[13] This, too, has implications for school science, for children, too, can be imprisoned in this way by their preconceptions, observing the world through their own particular 'conceptual spectacles'.

The implications of paying more than lip service to this constructivist view of science are explored in some detail throughout the book. Here I will illustrate some main points with a couple of classroom examples. The first example illustrates the hypothetico-deductive nature of science enquiries. It shows an investigation taking place, not from observation to generalization, but being initiated by a hypothesis which in this case derives from a pupil's alternative framework.

Two 11-year-old boys, Tim and Ricky, are doing simple experiments on the extension of springs when loaded. They have made their own spring by winding wire round a length of dowel. One end of the spring is supported in a clamp and a polystyrene cup is hanging from the other end (Figure 1, p.6). Following instructions, they investigate the extension of the spring as they add ball bearings to the polystyrene cup. Ricky is adding the ball bearings one at a time and measuring the new length of the spring after each addition. Tim is watching him, then interrupts:

> How far is that off the ground? Pull it up and see
> if the spring does not move any.

He unclamps the spring, raises it higher up the stand, and again measures its length. Apparently satisfied that the length is the same, he continues with the experiment. Later, when he was asked the reason for doing this, he explained that he

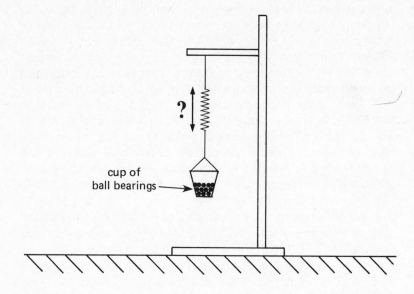

cup of
ball bearings ⟶

Figure 1

thought the weight of the cup of ball bearings would increase
if it were raised. To explain his reasoning, he picked up two
marbles and held one up higher than the other:

> This is farther up and gravity is pulling it down
> harder—I mean the gravity is still the same but it
> turns out it is pulling harder the farther away. The
> higher it gets the more effect gravity will have on it
> because, like if you just stood over there and some-
> one dropped a pebble on him, it would just sting
> him, it wouldn't hurt him. But like if I dropped it
> from an aeroplane it would be accelerating faster
> and faster and when it hit someone on the head it
> would kill him.

It appears that Tim's idea of weight encompasses the notion
of potential energy and leads him to predict a greater extension of the spring when it is further from the ground. He uses
the same framework when considering the force required to
hold a trolley at different positions on an inclined board,

predicting that it will be harder to hold when it is higher up than when it is lower down the slope.

Not only does this example indicate how pupils' alternative frameworks can intrude into their activities in science lessons, it illustrates how, in some cases, alternative frameworks are more than an idiosyncratic response to a particular task, they may be general notions applied to a range of situations.

There is evidence from a number of investigations that pupils have common alternative frameworks in a range of areas including physical phenomena such as the propagation of light, simple electrical circuits, ideas about force and motion and chemical change, also biological ideas concerned with growth and adaptation.

It follows from a constructivist philosophy of science that theory is not related in a deductive, and hence unique, way to observations; there can be multiple explanations of events which each account for the data. In the example of Tim's idea of weight we see how he had developed an idea based on common experiences with falling objects, yet he had explained them to himself in a way that differed from the accepted physicist's view. The possibility of multiple interpretations of an event is also illustrated in the following example of work done in a science class of 12-year-old pupils. A pair of girls were doing an experiment in which an immersion heater was placed in blocks of different metals, each of the same weight (Figure 2, p.8). The pupils had been instructed on a worksheet to draw a temperature-time graph for each block as it was heated. The purpose of the experiment being to illustrate variation in specific heat capacities of different metals. The girls had chosen blocks of iron and aluminium, and towards the end of the lesson they were instructed to look at their graphs, compare them and suggest explanations for any differences. Here are their comments:

P1: We've got to do a graph for the aluminium.
P2: Good. Aluminium isn't so—um—it—
P1: Don't forget it has to go through, doesn't it? Through the thickness to reach there—the thermometer.
P2: That was only thin to get to that.
P1: Come on, we've got to put it away now.

The teacher enters the discussion.

T: What has your experiment shown you?
P2: That different—um—that different materials and that see how heat could travel through them.
T: What did you find out?
P1: Well—er—that heat went through the—the iron more easier than it did through the—er—
P2: Aluminium.

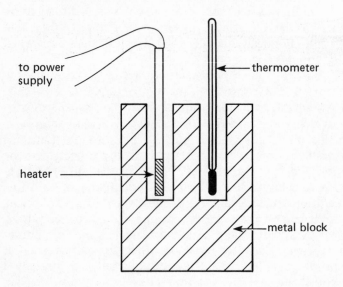

to power supply

thermometer

heater

metal block

Figure 2

Here pupils had performed the experiment and had collected their data, yet it appears from their comments that they interpreted the difference between the graphs for the two metal blocks not in terms of the amount of heat required to raise the temperature of each by a certain amount, but in terms of the comparative conductivity of metals.

The more simplistic interpretations of the discovery approach in science suggest that we only need to give pupils the opportunity to explore events and phenomena at first hand and they will be able to induce the generalizations and principles themselves. The position suggested here is that children do make generalizations from their firsthand experiences, but these may not be the ones the teacher has in mind. Explanations do not spring clearly or uniquely from data.

Through the eyes of those initiated in the currently accepted theories of science, common school demonstrations, such as trolleys and ticker tapes, experiments with batteries and bulbs, or work with ray boxes, mirrors and prisms, appear to offer self-sufficient support for the underlying principles they are designed to demonstrate, whether it is Newton's Laws of Motion or the Laws of Reflection of Light. If children fail to abstract and understand these principles from their experiments, it may be seen as the children's error either for not observing accurately or not thinking logically about the pattern in the results.

The constructivist view of science, on the other hand, indicates the fallacy here. If we wish children to develop an understanding of the conventional concepts and principles of science, more is required than simply providing practical experiences. The theoretical models and scientific conventions will not be 'discovered' by children through their practical work. They need to be presented. Guidance is then needed to help children assimilate their practical experiences into what is possibly a new way of thinking about them.

The slogan 'I do and I understand' is commonly used in support of practical work in science teaching. We have classrooms where activity plays a central part. Pupils can spend a major portion of their time pushing trolleys up runways, gathering, cutting and sticking tangling metres of ticker tape; marbles are rattled around in trays simulating solids, liquids and gases, batteries and bulbs are clicked in and out of specially designed circuit boards. To what end? In many classrooms, I suspect, 'I do and I am even more confused'.

This process of 'making sense' takes on even greater significance when considering children's alternative frameworks. Not only do children have to comprehend the new model or principle being presented to them, but they have to make the intellectual leap of possibly abandoning an alternative framework which until that time had worked well for them.

To use the language of philosophy of science, children sometimes need to undergo paradigm shifts in their thinking. Max Planck suggested that new theories do not convert people, it is just that old men die. If scientists have this difficulty in reformulating their conceptions of the world, is it a wonder that children sometimes have a struggle to do so?

References

1. J. S. Bruner, *The Process of Education*, Random House (1963).
2. D. P. Ausubel, *Educational Psychology: A Cognitive View*, Holt, Reinhart (1968).
3. *Nuffield Physics Teachers' Guide*, No. 1, Longmans/Penguin (1966).
4. R. Driver, The name of the game, *Sch. Sci. Rev.*, **56**, 800–5 (1975).
5. J. J. Wellington, 'What's supposed to happen, sir?': some problems with discovery learning, *Sch. Sci. Rev.*, **63**, 163–73 (1981).
6. An account of current aspects of the philosophy and sociology of science is given in *What is Science?*, ASE Study series, No. 15 (1979).
7. K. R. Popper, *Objective Knowledge*, OUP (1972).
8. M. Polanyi, *Personal Knowledge*, Routledge (1958).
9. T. Kuhn, *The Structure of Scientific Revolutions*, Chicago (1963).
10. I. Lakatos, *Criticism and the Growth of Knowledge*, CUP (1974).
11. J. Ziman, *Public Knowledge*, CUP (1968).
12. N. R. Hanson, *Patterns of Discovery*, CUP (1958).
13. K. Popper, Normal science and its dangers, I. Lakatos and A. Musgrave (eds.), in *Criticism and the Growth of Knowledge*.

2

LEARNING TO OBSERVE

Enter a laboratory; approach the table crowded with an assortment of apparatus, an electric cell, silk-covered copper wire, small cups of mercury, spools, a mirror mounted on an iron bar; the experimenter is inserting into small openings the metal ends of ebony-headed pins; the iron oscillates and the mirror attached to it throws a luminous band upon a celluloid scale. The forward—backward motion of this spot enables the physicist to observe the minute oscillations of the iron bar. But ask him what he is doing. Will he answer 'I am studying the oscillations of an iron bar which carries a mirror'? No, he will say that he is measuring the electric resistance of the spools. If you are astonished, if you ask him what the words mean, what relation they have with the phenomena he has been observing and which you have noted at the same time as he, he will answer that your question requires a long explanation and that you should take a course in electricity.

P. Duhem, *The Aim and Structure of Physical Theory*, Philip P. Weiner Trans. (1962).

This passages illustrates how a naive observer of an electrical experiment sees various aspects of the apparatus: ebony-headed pins, cups of mercury, a mirror, a celluloid scale. Yet without the conceptual framework of the physicist he cannot discriminate between the relevant and the irrelevant aspects. Nor does he understand how they relate together.

One of the reasons commonly given for teaching science in schools is that it trains pupils to be observant, to be objective and precise in their reporting and recording of events. But as this quotation from Duhem illustrates, different people looking at the same thing may be perceiving it rather differently. 'Looking at' is not a passive recording of an image like a photograph being produced by a camera, but it is

an active process in which the observer is checking his perceptions against his expectations.

When children are asked to make observations in the
course of their work in science it is apparent that at times
they see what they expect to see. The record they make of
their observations either by writing or drawing indicates their
understanding of the phenomenon. As with the naive observer
in the physics laboratory, children do not know what aspects
of a situation to pay attention to and which to ignore.

Through the microscope

Many teachers will be familiar with the experience of helping
pupils see what they 'ought' to see through a microscope.
Children viewing a biological cell through a microscope for
the first time produce drawings which show not only that
some have difficulty identifying what are the significant
features, but they painstakingly record irrelevant ones, such
as air bubbles.

Smoke cells and Brownian motion

This beautiful piece of evidence for the existence of molecular motion is commonly presented to schoolchildren. One
class was instructed on how to use the smoke cells and asked
to draw and write about what they saw explaining their
observations.

Figures 3- -5 (pp. 14, 15) show a selection of children's
reports. As well as being a very obvious reminder of the range
in quality of written work that 14-year-old pupils produce,
the reports contain other interesting features, especially in
the explanations pupils give for their observations.

While the children were doing the activity, the teacher
was circulating and talking about the observations made. The
phrase 'random motion' was injected into the discussion by
him, and we see this picked up and used in all the reports. It
is the children's reasons for this 'random motion' which are
interesting to note.

When smoke particles collide and move in different
directions we call this random motion.

The smoke particles collide with each other and molecules of air.

Some children clearly thought the sudden changes in direction of the smoke particles were produced by collisions between them. The teacher saw some of the children writing this down and asked the class how many of them thought this and how many thought they changed direction without bumping into one another. The class was about equally divided between the two. They were then instructed to return to their microscopes and look carefully to see which of the alternatives actually happens. This time the pupils returned with a purpose to their observation, and the matter was resolved.

Until there is a clear question to answer by observation children may not record what they see carefully. In a class of 11-year-olds the children were making drawings of a woodlouse from specimens in front of them. The teacher approaches one group and looks over the children's shoulders to see the drawings of oval segmented bodies with protruding legs. He counts the legs on one drawing, then those on another. 'Seven, eight, ten ... are you all looking at the same woodlouse? How many legs *does* it have?' Again, the children's attention was focused by comparing their record of observations. They repeated their drawings, this time not simply looking *at* the woodlouse, but looking *for* specific features. Careful observation of biological specimens can be encouraged by asking a group of children to decide which drawing is most faithful to the specimen. Features which some have omitted are pointed out and discussion of the selection of relevant and irrelevant features is stimulated.

Iron filings and magnets

The drawing of biological specimens is just one example of pupils being asked to observe a pattern or regularity when they are not quite clear what they are looking for. In these situations they have to be educated into what to see; to distinguish between relevant and irrelevant aspects of a phenomenon. Children's initial observations of patterns in iron filings around magnets are such an example.

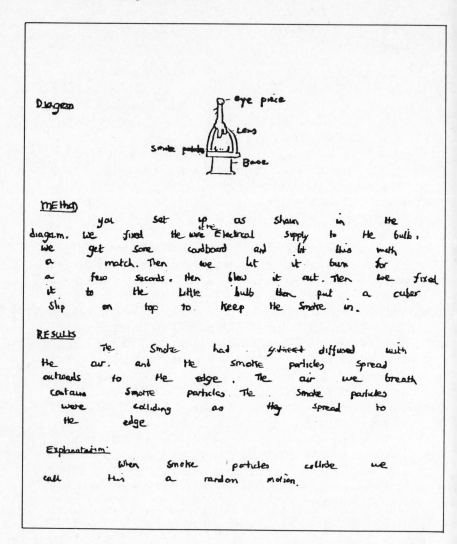

Diagram

Method

you set up as shown in the diagram. We fixed it re the wire Electrical supply to He bulb. We get some cardboard and lit this meth a match. Then we lit it burn for a few seconds. Then blew it out. Then we fixed it to the little bulb then put a cuber slip on top to keep the smoke in.

Results

The smoke had y.treet diffused with the air. and the smoke particles spread outwards to the edge. The air we breath contains smoke particles The smoke particles were colliding as they spread to the edge.

Explanation

When smoke particles collide we call this a random motion.

Figure 3

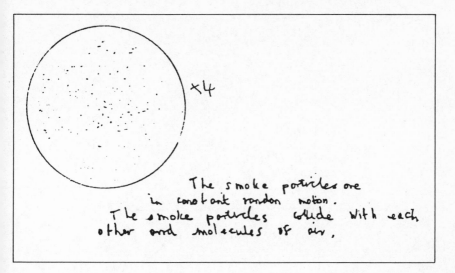

The smoke particles are in constant random motion.
The smoke particles collide with each other and molecules of air.

Figure 4

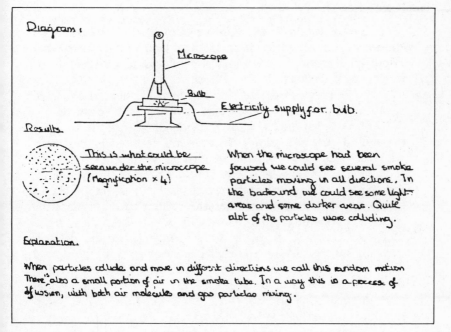

Diagram:

Microscope

Bulb

Electricity supply for bulb.

Results.

This is what could be seen under the microscope (Magnification x 4)

When the microscope had been focused we could see several smoke particles moving in all directions. In the background we could see some light areas and some darker areas. Quite a lot of the particles were colliding.

Explanation.

When particles collide and move in different directions we call this random motion. There's also a small portion of air in the smoke tube. In a way this is a process of diffusion, with both air molecules and gas particles mixing.

Figure 5

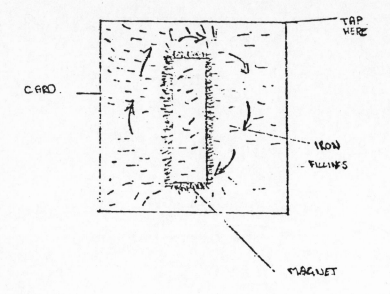

Figure 6

Figures 6 and 7 show drawings made by two boys from the same class. Figure 6 is an attempt by a boy to show what appeared significant to him. Obviously, the outline of the magnet was clear from the pattern of iron filings. But it was also the *movement* of the filings when he tapped the card that caught his attention and was recorded in the drawing.

The other figure (Figure 7) shows a boy's sketch of the pattern in the iron filings. In this case the heavy lines were superimposed by the teacher in correcting the work.

This is a case where it is not to be expected that children will see the representation the teacher has drawn. 'Lines of force' are physicists' constructs, they do not describe what is happening to the iron filings. Rather, they are a convenient way of relating theory and observation. Perhaps it is no surprise that children's drawings do not correspond well with the teacher's representations. The connection between the actual pattern in the filings and its conventional representation in terms of 'lines of force' is one which children have to be trained to use. Figures 8 and 9 show the development of one child's perception of this. Figure 8 shows his initial attempts to represent the pattern around a single

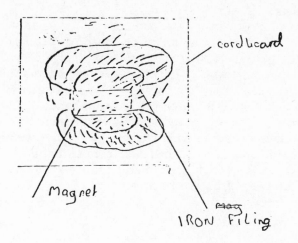

cord board

Magnet

IRON Filing

Figure 7

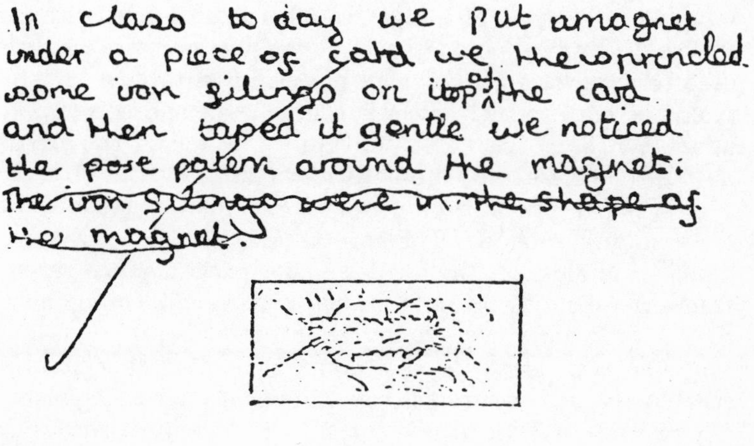

In class to day we put a magnet
under a piece of card we the sprinckled
some ion filings on it op the card
and then taped it gentle we noticed
the pose patern around the magnet.
The ion filings were in the shape of
the magnet.

Figure 8

magnet. There is evidence of some pattern there, but it is far from clear.

When most of the class had completed this drawing, the teacher placed a magnet on an overhead projector and indicated the pattern to look for in the iron filings. The children were then told to make drawings of the patterns they saw using two magnets with opposing, then similar, poles facing each other. Figure 9 shows the drawings made by the same child of the patterns in the iron filings showing how he has become more aware of the conventional way of representing the pattern and is extending his representation of it. The drawings with the field lines marked on them are his copies of the teacher's blackboard diagrams.

Ripple tanks

The patterns of waves in ripple tanks usually appeal to children. The changing forms and colours intrigue and fascinate. However, children do have difficulty in recording what they observe.

A simple task with the ripple tank is to observe the reflection of plane waves from a straight barrier. When the waves strike the barrier at an angle the wave pattern produced is quite complex. Some children in recording their observations show the reflected wave at right angles to the incident wave for all angles of incidence. This is a case, as with the smoke cell, when looking again at the phenomenon could be used to advantage. In complex patterns like those in a ripple tank it is hard to pick out salient features; children's expectations can dominate their perceptions. Some of the effects may also be masked by more obvious features.

When two point sources were used, one boy recorded his observations as shown in Figure 10 (p.20). The activity was designed to illustrate the formation of an interference pattern where waves superimpose. This boy's drawing did not indicate these clearly and the work had to be 'corrected'.

The complex patterns produced in ripple tanks are not easy to see and sometimes even more difficult to represent. Figure 11 (p.21) shows one particularly striking attempt by a 14-year-old to capture the pattern he saw.

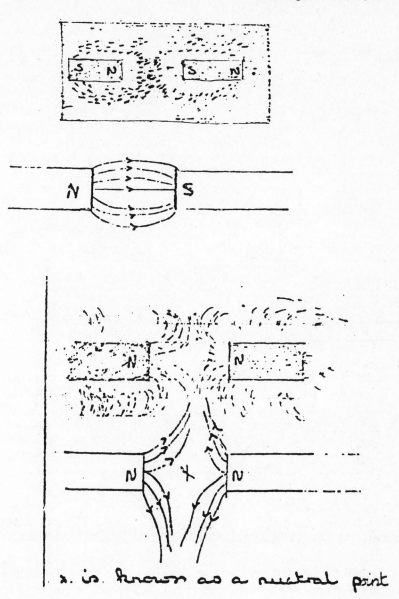

x. is known as a neutral point

Figure 9

The waves. overlap. each other

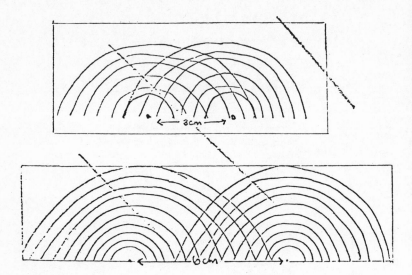

Figure 10

The drawings of iron filings and ripple patterns are examples of cases where the diagrams are expected to follow certain conventions which cannot be learned from the phenomenon itself. Instruction in such agreed conventions is necessary; children have to be told about them.

Refraction and the rainbow

We have already seen several examples of cases where children's expectations affected their drawings. A very clear example of this occurred in an introductory lesson on the properties of light with a group of 15-year-olds. They were working in groups, each with a ray box and a selection of mirrors, lenses and prisms. They were to record what each device did to the light. Figures 12 and 13 (p.22) are the record made by two pupils.

WAVES CROSSING

(a) We set up the ripple tank and started a pulse with one finger and then straight afterwards side started with another finger

(s) We used both fingers then and froze them with a stroboscope

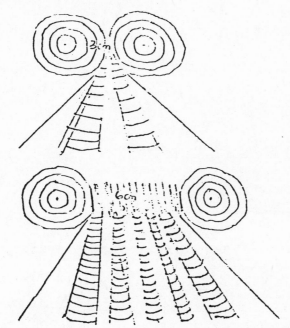

Figure 11

The pupils had clearly seen the coloured light produced and noticed that it went a different way from the incident beam: but a curved path? In this case, is it that the pupils' ideas of coloured light and rainbows affected what was drawn?

The second drawing on reflection, apart from other problems the pupil had with it, indicates another quite commonly held idea that mirrors reflect light in a direction normal to their surface.

In summary, then, what pupils record as their observations in science activities depends on a range of factors.

First, their observations may be focused by their preconceptions or expectations, as in the case of the drawings of patterns in ripple tanks or of smoke cells. The teacher's task

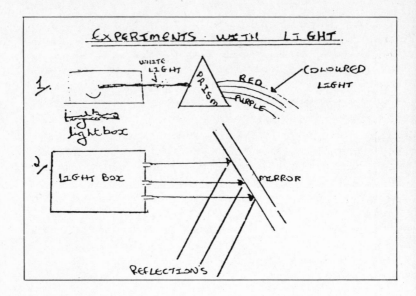

Figure 12

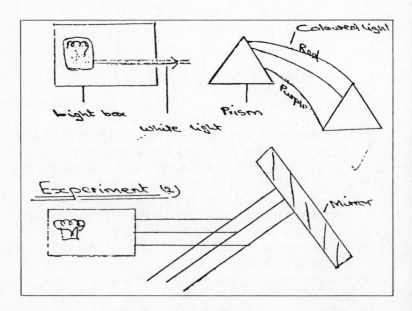

Figure 13

in such cases is to encourage pupils to look again, check their observations, perhaps comparing them with one another, until the unexpected is clearly seen.

There are also cases where pupils are observing complex phenomena and are not clear as to which features to focus on. This was the problem in the drawings of living cells and the patterns of iron filings. In cases like this, the teacher who knows what the activity is designed to illustrate can help pupils sort out relevant from irrelevant features by directing their observations. The examples of focused observations being developed during the lesson on magnetic fields and Brownian motion are useful illustrations of a teacher's influence here.

Lastly, in some cases pupils are expected to make the record of their observations using certain conventions, whether they be the conventions of lines of force or rays of light. These may not faithfully represent the phenomenon and clearly have to be taught rather than 'discovered'.

3

MAKING MEANINGS

. . . preconceptions are amazingly tenacious and resistant to
extinction . . . the unlearning of preconceptions might well
prove to be the most determinative single factor in the
acquisition and retention of subject-matter knowledge.
Ausubel (1968).

Analogy and understanding

Pupils, particularly younger adolescents, are rarely slow to
suggest reasons for unexpected and interesting phenomena.
Most science teachers will have a fund of interesting or
unorthodox ideas pupils have put forward in their lessons.

In an introductory lesson on electrostatics with some
13-year-old boys, a teacher brought in a balloon. After inflat-
ing it, he rubbed it on his sleeve and held it over some small
pieces of paper, which fluttered around on the bench.

'What makes that happen?' he asks. A shower of
hands goes up.
'Please sir, is it that when you rub the balloon you
let a little air out and it blows the paper around?'

Such ideas are often readily suggested by pupils and it
is not surprising that in many cases they do not correspond
with the accepted answer. Within the limits of the pupils'
experience the suggestions may be quite reasonable. Faced
with a novel phenomenon, pupils are searching to find familiar
events to which they can relate this new experience. They
try to interpret the unfamiliar by analogy with familiar
experiences.

A common introductory experiment in electrostatics is

for pupils to note the attraction between rubbed strips of perspex and polythene. It is quite common for pupils to spontaneously test both ends of the rubbed strip 'to see if it works like a magnet'.

At the end of a lesson in which pupils had seen a coin and a feather both fall down at the same rate in an evacuated tube, a pupil came up to the teacher:

> Is that why there is no gravity on the moon? There is no air to push things down?

Here the more mysterious phenomenon, that of gravity, was being assimilated into the more familiar and concrete experience of air pressure.

All the ideas discussed so far are attempts by pupils to understand new events by relating them to what they already know. They are ideas they are prepared to 'try out for size'. Usually, they are transitory and quickly abandoned in the face of contrary evidence or alternative explanations.

Some ideas or alternative frameworks are much more deep-seated. Unlike the kinds of examples discussed already, which may be idiosyncratic suggestions by individual pupils, aspects of these more deep-seated frameworks are common to the thinking of many children.

Commonly held alternative frameworks

In the main, studies of children's conceptual understanding in science have tended to focus on the proportion of pupils of different ages who give the accepted or 'right' answers to questions. The possibility of finding out important information by also studying patterns in types of 'errors' has tended to be a more recent development.

Several studies have been reported which list a catalogue of errors or common misconceptions about natural phenomena. In a study of Lebanese school and university students[1] twenty common misconceptions in the areas of physics, Earth science, chemistry and biology are reported. Other studies[2,3] indicate the existence of misconceptions which appear to be as prevalent among students studying science as those who do not.

Such 'catalogues' are useful pointers to problem areas, but they tend to trivialize the nature of the problem by giving the impression that the source of errors are mislearned 'facts'. In some cases the errors may be superficial in character, in that they can easily be corrected by teaching. However, in many cases the source of particular errors derives from pupils' having very different models or alternative frameworks from those of the scientific community.

In order to investigate such alternative frameworks, pupils' thinking has to be probed in some detail; it is the reasons pupils give for their answers, not the answers themselves, that are important.

The ways that younger children explain and interpret certain natural events were explored by Jean Piaget in his well-known early works[4],[5] in which he asked children such questions as, 'What causes night?', 'How do clouds move?' and 'Which of these objects is alive?' These studies have been extensively replicated[6] and the results are still worth scrutiny in terms of the ideas children of different ages suggest. One might ask, for example, what implications it might have for introductory biology courses if one takes seriously the finding that over ten per cent of 11-year-olds in Britain extend their concept of 'living things' to include the sun, wind and fire.[7]

One area in which alternative frameworks are common and persistent is that of dynamics. An example is given in the following discussion with 11-year-old Jane about what makes a ball bearing stop as it rolls along the floor.

> I don't know. Why do they stop? It's just they always stop. After you push it they go as far as the push . . . how hard it was and after that wears off it just goes back like it used to be.'

Here Jane seems to consider the natural state of any object to be the stationary state, and when the initial impetus given to the ball is used up it returns to this state.

Later, Jane is doing an experiment with another pupil, Cathy, pulling objects along a horizontal surface with a spring balance to see how much force is required. They had already suggested that the force would depend on the speed at which the objects are pulled and the teacher had supplied them with a small motorized vehicle to use in their tests so as to maintain a constant speed. They have measured the force required to drag a range of blocks over the surface and now they connect the spring balance to a dynamics trolley:

Jane: OK, here goes. Read it as it comes by you.
Cathy: Oh, I can't.
Jane: Um—zero! Gosh, it doesn't take anything to pull that—it says—watch this—zero! It can't do that. Try it backwards and forwards again.
Cathy: OK. It's zero.

The girls accept the result but do not understand it. This is apparent when they do a further experiment and record the motion of a trolley when it is pulled by a constant force. To do this, the girls use a drip cup tied to the back of the trolley to indicate how far it goes in equal intervals of time.

Teacher: What do you think will happen when you pull this along with the same force?
Jane: The drips will be the same distance apart.
Cathy: Now you keep it at a steady reading.
Jane: I'll do 100 first (referring to the reading in grammes weight on the spring balance).
Cathy: OK, go!

The girls measure the distance between the drips with a ruler.

Cathy: 8½, 16½, 19½.
Jane: Don't you do it between each one?
Cathy: We *are* doing it between each one.
Jane: It gets faster and faster!
Cathy: Yea.
Jane: (calling to the teacher as he passes) See! This one was 8½, then 16½ and 19½. Even though the force was the same, they get faster and faster. It shouldn't do that, should it?

It is clear that the girls were expecting a constant force to result in the trolley moving with constant speed. They were surprised and mistrusting of the results they obtained which indicated that the trolley went for increasingly greater distances in equal time intervals.

Similar Aristotelian ideas about motion have been

reported by Piaget[8] and have even been shown to persist in the problem-solving approaches of university physics students. Viennot[9] investigated the responses of several hundred school and university students to problems related to force and motion. She reports the existence of types of 'spontaneous reasoning' which persist despite instruction. In particular, her study identified in students' reasoning the existence of two notions of forces, one associated with accelerated motion, the other with velocity, a notion similar to impulse or to 'impetus' in pre-Galilean dynamics. In problems involving opposing forces, students tended to suggest that 'when there is motion, the action exceeds the reaction (or vice versa), the resultant force being in the direction of motion'. Similar results are reported by Sjøberg and Lie[10] who gave written problems on dynamics to over 400 16—19-year-old upper secondary school students in Norway. (Students in teacher training colleges and universities were also included in the study.) Evidence for Aristotelian thinking was found in all groups of students. The authors also report a tendency for students to associate gravity with the existence of an atmosphere.

Pupils' notions about heat also exhibit commonly held alternative frameworks. These indicate that many pupils, even throughout secondary schooling, regard heat as a kind of substance endowed with a motive force.

In the following passage we see how three 12-year-old pupils interpret what they observe when a balloon on a tin can gets bigger as the tin is heated gently.

Nigel: What do you think will happen, Kevin?
Kevin: I think it will—erm—blow up and—er—pop with the force of the heat.
Nigel: But where's the force coming from?
Kevin: From bottom going through that (points to can) then—erm . . .
Nigel: What do you think, Susan?
Susan: The heat's coming and it's collecting in that can and it's blowing the bubble up.
Nigel: Well there is air in there at first. And the heat get into it and it's rising up and it's making the balloon bigger.
Teacher: So what's pushing the balloon out?

All: The air inside the can.
Teacher: How does the air do that?
Nigel: The heat's pushing the air so it blows the
         balloon up.
Teacher: What's it making the air do, this heat?
Susan: Rise.
Nigel: Force up—it's forcing it up.

The first statement made by Kevin referred to the 'force of the heat'. Susan follows this with the suggestion that 'heat's coming and collecting in that can'. Both the statements reflect the idea of heat as the active agent. It is the heat that acts directly on the balloon. Nigel is the first to mention air, although from his statement it appears that he does not consider the air as expanding in all directions, rather that the heat is pushing the air up.

Pupils' ideas about heat have been studied in some detail by Erickson.[11] He interviewed Canadian pupils between the ages of 6 and 13, and has constructed a conceptual inventory of commonly held ideas about the composition of heat (e.g. there are two types of heat—hot heat and cold heat), the movement of heat, the effects of heat and heat and temperature.

Andersson[12] gave 12—15-year-old Swedish children written problems concerning the boiling point of water. His results indicate that a considerable proportion of pupils have not made the distinction between heat and temperature. Problems in understanding the intensive nature of temperature are also reported in a study by Strauss.[13] In a series of tasks, he asks pupils to predict the final temperature produced on mixing two containers of water. His results indicate an interesting trend. The youngest children tend to use their qualitative judgement and, for example, in predicting the resultant temperature when two containers of water at the same initial temperature are mixed, will give the correct response. Older children will begin to pay attention to the numbers in the problem and suggest that the resultant temperature will be the sum of the two initial temperatures. By mid-adolescence, pupils are again giving the correct answer. Strauss reports similar U-shaped curves for children's performance in other tasks involving intensive quantities.

Pupils' understanding of the particulate theory of matter has been investigated with 14-year-old Israeli children.[14] After being taught the topic, nearly half the pupils tended to use a model based on continuous matter, rather than particulate theory, to explain simple phenomena involving gases.

A series of studies has been undertaken in Scotland on selected conceptual areas in chemistry which indicate learning difficulties arising in the course of teaching specific topics. In a study of the mole concept[15] the difficulties of 14—15-year-old pupils following an O-grade syllabus were studied. Three areas of difficulty were reported including, for example, the common misapprehension that one mole of a compound will always react with one mole of another. In a study of thermodynamic ideas of older students (aged 16—18 years) in Scotland[16] eight major misconceptions were identified, including the idea that reactions have to be exothermic to be spontaneous.

Studies of alternative frameworks have also been undertaken in biology. A study, also undertaken in Scotland,[17] reports a range of ideas which biology pupils have in connection with plant growth. Of particular interest and concern is the proportion of O-grade pupils who, despite instruction in photosynthesis, claim that 'most of the food of a green plant is obtained from the soil'. A study of English secondary school boys' thinking about adaptation and evolution[18] indicates the strong tendency of pupils to think in Lamarckian terms.

Studies of children's ideas about light,[19] electricity,[20] air pressure[21] and astronomical notions[22] have also been reported. It is not possible in a short book to do justice to the detail in any of these studies. However, the general picture that emerges is of a considerable number of secondary pupils holding on to certain intuitive notions despite the science teaching they receive in school.

References

1. G. J. Za'rour, Interpretation of natural phenomena by Lebanese school children, *Sci. Educ.*, **60**, 227—97 (1976).

2. L. J. Koethe, Science concepts: a study of 'sophisticated' errors, *Sci. Educ.*, **47**, 361—4 (1963).

3. C. A. Boyd, A study of unfounded beliefs, *Sci. Educ.*, **50**, 396—8 (1966).

4. J. Piaget, *The Child's Conception of the World*, Harcourt Brace (1929).

5. J. Piaget, *The Child's Conception of Physical Causality*, Routledge (1930).

6. M. Laurendeau and A. Pinard, *Causal Thinking in the Child*, International University Press (1962).

7. W. H. King, Symposium: studies of children's scientific concepts and interests, *Brit. J. Educ. Psychol.*, **31**, 1—20 (1961).

8. J. Piaget, *Understanding Causality*, Norton (1974).

9. L. Viennot, Spontaneous reasoning in elementary dynamics, *Eur. J. Sci. Educ.*, **1**, 205—22 (1979).

10. S. Sjøberg and S. Lie, Ideas about force and movement among Norwegian pupils and students, Report 81—11, Institute of Physics Report Series, University of Oslo.

11. G. Erickson, Children's conceptions of heat and temperature, *Sci. Educ.*, **60**, 221—30 (1976).

12. B. Andersson, Some aspects of children's understanding of boiling point, in W. F. Archenhold, R. H. Driver, A. Orton and C. Wood-Robinson (eds.) *Cognitive Development Research in Science and Mathematics*, University of Leeds (1980).

13. S. Strauss, Educational implications of U-shaped behavioural growth, a position paper for the Ford Foundation, Tel-Aviv University, 1977.

14. S. Novick and J. Nussbaum, Junior high school pupils' understanding of the particulate nature of matter: an interview study, *Sci. Educ.*, **62**, 273—82 (1978).

15. I. M. Duncan and A. H. Johnstone, The mode concept, *Educ. Chem.*, **10**, 213—14 (1973).

16. A. H. Johnstone, J. J. MacDonald and G. Webb, A thermodynamic approach to chemical equilibrium, *Phys. Educ.*, **12**, 248—51 (1977).

17. B. Arnold and M. Simpson, An investigation of the development of the concept Photosynthesis to SCE O Grade, Aberdeen College of Education (1980).

18. J. A. Deadman and P. J. Kelly, What do secondary school boys understand about evolution and heredity before they are taught the topics?' *J. Biol. Educ.*, **12**, 7—15 (1978).

19. E. Guesne, 'Lumière et vision des objets: un exemple de représent- ations des phénomènes physiques préexistant à l'enseignment', in *Proceedings of GIREP*, Taylor & Francis (1976).

20. D. Wilkinson, A study of some concepts involving electricity, MA Thesis, University of Leeds (1973).

21. E. Engel and R. Driver, 'Investigating pupils' understanding of aspects of pressure', in *Proceedings of the international work- shop on Problems Concerning Students' Representation of Physics and Chemistry Knowledge*, Ludwigsburg, 1981.

22. J. Nussbaum and J. Novak, An assessment of children's concepts of the Earth utilising structured interviews, *Sci. Educ.*, **60**, 535—50 (1976).

4

CHILDREN'S BELIEFS
AND CLASSROOM LEARNING

The last chapter indicated that pupils may have some strongly held ideas or beliefs about the phenomena they study in science lessons. These ideas influence the observations pupils make in their experiments, as well as affecting the explanations they give for them. They can also persist in a range of situations and be resistant to change. It is to these influences on pupils' classroom learning that I now turn.

When pupils undertake investigations with unfamiliar equipment, their explorations may include what appear to be irrelevant tests.

Tim and Carl were performing a sequence of tasks with a simple balance (Figure 14, p.34) made of a sheet of pegboard suspended from a nail on a stand. Washers were used as weights and were hooked on with paper clips. The boys had worked through a sequence of experiments related to the law of moments.

As an extra exercise, it was suggested they hang a weight over a pulley, attach it to one end of the balance beam, and see if they can make a rule to predict how to keep the beam level. They set up the apparatus, and Carl starts by hanging two washers on the hook over the pulley and two on the hook underneath it. The beam balances. Tim then notices that the pulley is composed of three concentric wheels of different diameters. He moves the string across on to each of the wheels in turn to see if this makes a difference. Carl follows by moving the hook on the peg-board vertically up

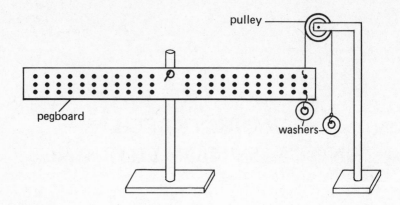

Figure 14

to see if that affects the balance. Both these last manoeuvres could be considered by a physicist as irrelevant, yet the boys needed to test them out.

It is easy in teaching to prescribe a specific sequence of activities in order to substantiate a principle of law. With the hindsight of experience and training what the teacher may not be aware of are the avenues of exploration which the pupils have to undertake to satisfy themselves. They may need to test out some ideas if only to reject them.

In an investigation of pupils' learning about flotation, Cole and Raven[1] studied the effect of pupils' exploration of irrelevant variables on learning. They compare the learning of two groups of pupils. One undertook only experiments which focused on relevant aspects of the problem (such as the density of the objects and the liquid). The other, in addition had the opportunity to explore irrelevant aspects, such as the depth of the water. Overall, the second group performed better on the final test, which involved applying what was learned to new problems.

As well as influencing the investigation of 'irrelevant' aspects of a system, pupils' frameworks or expectations may also cause the neglect of relevant features. The pupils' accounts of Brownian motion discussed earlier indicated that some pupils failed to see the important feature of the motion of the smoke particles, that they appear to change direction without colliding with a visible agent.

Returning to the topic of dynamics, it is noticeable that, until the idea is specifically introduced to them, many pupils fail to observe accelerated motion.

Before doing some class experiments, Tim was asked to predict what would happen when two dynamics carts were pushed apart by a spring loaded plunger in one of them. One of the carts had two bricks on it. He correctly predicted that the lighter cart would go faster. He was asked to sketch a graph (Figure 15) of how the speeds of the carts changed from the moment the spring was released. When he was asked what happened to the speeds of the carts while the spring was pushing them, he responded, 'It happens immediately.' (After the teaching sequence, Tim was asked a similar question again. This time his graph did show the accelerating part of the motion.)

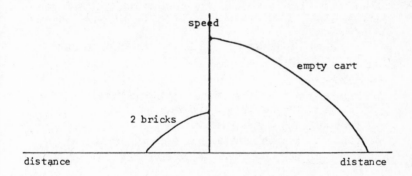

Figure 15

Earlier, it was indicated that pupils meeting a phenomenon for the first time, or a familiar one looked at in a new way, will try to relate it to an idea which is already understood, and explain it in those terms.

In Chapter 1, an example was given in which two girls explained the difference between two temperature—time graphs in terms of different rates of conduction. As the girls had not met the idea of heat capacity before, it is perhaps not so surprising that they interpreted the experiment in terms of more familiar ideas.

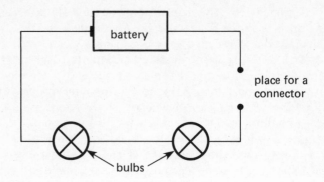

Figure 16

Early experiments with electricity and circuit boards are often interpreted by pupils in unorthodox ways, as the following excerpt suggests. Three 11-year-old boys were talking with their teacher about what to put into the gap in the circuit (Figure 16) to make the bulbs light up.*

Teacher: How am I going to get the bulb to light up?

Papu and
 Philip: By putting a connector in there, sir.

Papu: Sir, sir, they will divide, sir.

Teacher: What will divide?

Papu: Sir, the electricity, one will go that way, sir, and one will go this way, sir. Sir, it will be very dim.

Philip: 'Cos there is only one battery.

Teacher: Will they be as bright as each other, brighter or will one be brighter?

All: The same.

Philip: Sir, it's divided up the battery.

Papu: Sir, equal parts of the battery, sir, are divided up into the bulbs, sir, and the other, sir.

This passage indicates that one of the boys at least has the idea that electricity comes out of each end of the battery to light each bulb. This idea causes some difficulty when it is suggested that they add a third bulb to the circuit.

---

* Excerpt supplied by Peter Burton

Papu: Sir, but sir, it would be even dimmer than dimmer.

Philip: I think it would be right dim 'cos there's only one battery, and it's got to charge all them up.

Papu: Sir, it would have to split into thirds.

Paul: It can't. Don't be silly. It can't split up into thirds because there are only two ways out.

Papu: Sir, when you turn it on, sir, some of the electricity might go through the bulb, that bulb, sir, and into that bulb, sir.

The idea of electricity as going from each end of the battery to produce light in the bulbs is clearly evident here. It is only when the third bulb is introduced that the idea of some of the electricity actually passing through some of the circuit elements is suggested.

Even after a period of instruction, pupils' intuitions or alternative frameworks affect their thinking. In the next example we see how intuitions are involved when pupils are presented with a new problem and have to decide which principle or idea is relevant to its solution.

After a sequence of class work on the idea of 'forces in pairs', Jane was shown the apparatus (Figure 17). The weights were held in the position shown and Jane was asked to predict what would happen when they were released.

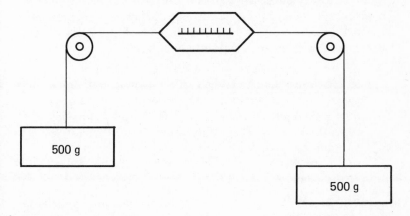

Figure 17

Jane: That will go down till they are both the same level.

Teacher: Why?

Jane: Well. This will start going down because they are the same weight—it will go at a speed, but so when it got level it couldn't stop so it would go up and down (indicates a balancing action with her hands) . . . sort of like a spring.

Jane is assimilating this new system into one she is already familiar with, a balancing system or bouncing spring. When she was shown what happened when the weights were released, she immediately changed her explanation.

Oh, I guess—well—they are still equal, so wherever they go they are still equal and won't move.

Although Jane appeared to understand the idea of equal and opposite forces, when faced with a new phenomenon she does not immediately use that idea in making her prediction, but rather sees the system in terms of a different analogy.

This is a common difficulty for pupils when they come to solve numerical problems. The difficulty is not so much the manipulative problems in handling the numbers or symbols, but deciding what principle is appropriate in the first place and how it related to the particular case in question. Thomas Kuhn suggests that exemplary problems help to shape pupils' perceptions of problem types and such exemplars play an important role in introducing pupils to the current scientific ideas. He points out that:

. . . the student discovers a way to see his problem as like a problem he has already encountered. Once that likeness or analogy has been seen, only manipulative difficulties remain . . . Students of physics regularly report that they have read through a chapter of their text, understood it perfectly, but none the less had difficulty in solving the problems at the chapter's end.[2]

Finally, even when pupils appear to have understood an idea or principle, they revert to alternate frameworks for their intuitions when faced with slightly novel tasks.

At the end of a teaching sequence on action and reaction, Ricky was asked to predict what would happen when two dynamics carts (one painted red, the other green) were pushed apart by a spring-loaded plunger. He predicted that:

> . . . the green cart will take off this way and the red *might* take off a little way this way, but—not as far as the green because the spring will have a force out this way and it's going to have another equal reactionary force, but that reactionary force still, for some reason—it's just as strong, but it doesn't have the same effect on it. Its effect isn't as strong.

In this statement we see that Ricky is aware of the problem as involving the principle of action and reaction and even recognizes that the two forces should be the same. However, his intuitions suggest that the cart doing the pushing should behave differently from the one being pushed, and ultimately in making his prediction he trusts his intuitions.

It has been suggested by some educators that misconceptions should be considered in designing instructional sequences; that it is as important to help pupils refute their misconceptions as it is to present the accepted view.

> . . . until one understands what pupils do spontaneously, one will not be able to demonstrate the limits of this approach to them.[3]

Teachers and curriculum developers could draw on some of the studies of pupils' alternative frameworks in creating teaching sequences which would challenge the ideas pupils are currently holding.[4] However, this approach is only possible if one is first aware of the nature of such alternative frameworks.

References

1. H. Cole and R. Raven, Principle learning as a function of instruction on excluding irrelevant variables, *J. Res. Sci. Teach.*, **6**, 234–42 (1969).
2. T. S. Kuhn, Second Thoughts on Paradigms, paper presented at the Illinois Symposium of Philosophy of Science, (1969).

3. R. Case, A Developmentally Based Theory and Technology of Instruction, The Ontario Institute for Studies in Education, Toronto (1976).

4. J. A. Rowell and C. J. Dawson, Teaching about floating and sinking: an attempt to link cognitive psychology with classroom practice, *Sci. Educ.*, **61**, 245–53 (1977).

5

INVENTION AND IMAGINATION

In certain areas of science (for example, dynamics, heat and electricity), there is evidence that pupils maintain aspects of their intuitions or alternative frameworks, especially when faced with problems in new contexts. Although science lessons may affect pupils' knowledge, more fundamental aspects of their thinking appear to be difficult to change. This obviously raises questions for science educators; how can a change in the way pupils conceptualize problems be encouraged?

It has already been indicated that giving pupils opportunities to refute their misconceptions, though it may be helpful, is not a complete answer. The alternative frameworks pupils have developed to interpret their experience have been built up over an extended period of time, and it is going to take more than one or two classroom activities to enable change to take place.

Further, an idea or framework will not be rejected until there is something adequate and reliable to replace it with. Pupils can be given experiences which conflict with their expectations, but those same experiences do not of themselves help the pupils to reconstruct an adequate alternative view of the system.

An example of such a situation was discussed in Chapter 3 where Jane and Cathy were surprised to find that it appeared to take no force to keep a cart rolling along a horizontal surface. In her written report on the sequence of experiments, Jane writes:

It took no force to pull a cart. Why? I don't understand (maybe a misreading).

Jane has done the experiment, collected the data, yet failed
to assimilate it into a new framework. Evidence and data can
be *discovered* but an interpretive framework is a construction
of the mind and has to be *invented*.

Sometimes pupils can invent frameworks which adequately account for the data, but many times, as with Jane,
they are left with a problem and no solution. In an article
entitled 'Discovery or invention', Atkin and Karplus[1] indicate
that many ideas basic to the sciences are constructs or inventions which have been shown to be powerful in explaining
and predicting events. Though pupils are creative in their
thinking, it is naive to suggest that they can be expected to
re-invent the important ideas of science. Atkin and Karplus
suggest that, instead, those ideas, whether about magnetic
fields or molecules, are presented by the teacher as inventions
and that pupils are then encouraged to see the value and
power of ideas by applying them in a range of activities.

This approach was used as a basis for the American
course, Science Curriculum Improvement Study (SCIS),[2]
designed for use with children aged 6—13. The teaching
materials are based on a three-phase learning cycle, which
includes the activities of *exploration, invention* and *discovery*.
In the first phase of the learning cycle for any idea or concept, pupils are allowed to explore a range of relevant phenomena for themselves; to extend their knowledge of relevant
aspects of the natural world. This phase is followed by an
input from the teacher, who introduces or 'invents' a new
concept or principle which will enable the pupils to organize
their experiences. In the third phase, the discovery phase,
pupils are given the opportunity to apply the concept to a
wide range of situations.

It is significant to note that in the SCIS course, which is
designed to cover 6 years of work, only twenty physical
science concepts are introduced. The teaching time is given to
the very important discovery phase.

It is tempting to think that in presenting pupils with a
new concept this will automatically become a powerful new
tool in their thinking. Pupils can memorize laws and principles, yet fail to apply them. In a discussion with Tim about

the motion of a ball bearing along a horizontal track:

Teacher: Why doesn't it go any farther?
Tim: Well, oh, we had this! Energy? I think it
         is kinetic energy (pause) is the only
         energy that is used up ... after a while
         the energy is gone so that makes the ball
         stop ... 'Cos you can't make or destroy
         energy except for this kinetic energy.

The law of conservation of energy is a powerful tool which, clearly, Tim had yet to learn how to use!

Kinetic molecular theory is another scientific idea which can easily be introduced too early or without enough time for consolidation. A class of 13-year-old pupils had completed a 6-week sequence of work on 'molecules in motion'. At the end they were given some homework to use the idea of the kinetic theory to explain a range of phenomena, including the expansion of mercury in a thermometer when it is heated. The following responses were among those that were given:

Mercury rises up a thermometer tube to get away from the heat. As soon as it has done (this) it stays till the heat has gone.

Mercury rises when it is heated because of a substance in the mercury that when heated is pushed up the thermometer.

Mercury rises up a thermometer when it is heated because it gets hot and the particles move away from the heat and up the thermometer.

Mercury likes to be cool so when it is heated the particles are trying to get away from the heat, so they move up as it's the only place it can go.

When mercury is heated it pushes the particle further away, thus the mercury's mass becomes bigger and it climbs up the thermometer giving a temperature reading.

Heat is making the particles expand, they now need more space to move and so push upwards making the mercury rise as well.

The first response does not refer to particles at all, but reflects an anthropomorphic interpretation of the mercury 'wanting to get away' from the heat. A similar idea is expressed in the third and fourth responses, although 'clothed' with the word 'particle'. The second response refers to a substance *in* the mercury. The idea that the particles of a substance are embedded in it like raisins in a teacake is a quite common notion. The sixth response shows a common misconception where the particles themselves are thought to expand.

The process of taking an idea presented by a teacher and using it in new contexts is far from straightforward. The following dialogue occurred in a science lesson with 13—14-year-old pupils. They had been presented with the ideas of the molecular—kinetic theory of matter and had been asked to use those ideas to explain some simple experiments, including the expansion of a metal rod on heating (Figure 18).

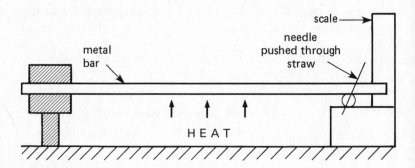

Figure 18

Yes, well that—the erm—the heat molecules are pushing the—
No, they're not.
Well, anyway, that thing's going down.
They're expanding. The—er—heat molecules are giving more energy so they need more room to move about and so the bar needs to get longer, so it goes down, the needle.
If that's the heat, and the molecules have to expand, right?—and you've got that thing like that, so when the molecules turn it round like that, and

when that bar pushes it, it pushes the things round
and that goes down.*

Again, we have an example of the idea of molecules expanding.
In addition, we see pupils using the idea of molecule to refer
to the heat—molecules of heat. The idea of the molecular—
kinetic theory may have been presented to the pupils, but it
needs careful consideration on their part to see how it applies
consistently to a range of experiences.

What is apparent in these examples is that they make a
demand on pupils' imaginative powers. They are asked to
explain the observable in terms of a model, the unobservable.
This requires the pupils to make mental constructions in
order to explain the events. The role of the imagination in
learning science is rarely emphasized, yet it probably plays
a very significant part in enabling pupils to grasp new ideas.

In his interesting critique of Bruner's *Man—A Course of
Study*, R. M. Jones emphasizes the importance of the imagination in the way pupils learn by assimilating new information
and accommodating their thinking to it.

It is important to bear in mind that in order for
this fundamental Piagetian principle to generate
optimum pedagogical power the elements of *significance and believability* must accrue to both the
unfamiliar and the familiar spheres. It is also
important to bear in mind ... the points of comparison which are potentially the most significant
are sometimes not immediately believable and
must first be made believable. *In other words,
children must sometimes imagine reality the better
to test it.*[3]

Before pupils can be expected to abandon their old ideas,
they have at least to be able to comprehend the ones which
are presented to them. This may involve an imaginative act
to consider the possibility of the new idea without necessarily
believing it to begin with.

The problems pupils have in understanding the laws of
motion have been indicated earlier. Even when the teacher

---

* Excerpt supplied by Mike Torbe.

demonstrated accelerated motion under a constant force, some pupils were unable to accept the idea. As one said,

> Of course, it is speeding up because you are pulling it faster and faster.

However, Ricky's comment on the experiment is very helpful in indicating how he explained the motion to himself:

> Oh, I see. It's like giving it a lot of pushes one after another and each one makes it go faster 'cos it doesn't slow down in between.

Here, he has constructed for himself the idea of a constant force as a series of impulses each of which adds an increment to the speed. On another occasion, Ricky shows imagination in clarifying the answer to a problem which arose in class discussion at the end of a teaching sequence on balancing and the law of moments. The teacher took a cardboard triangle and balanced it on his finger and asked the class what they could say about the point where his finger touched the cardboard.

Carl: All the weight is pushing down there.
Jane: It's the centre of gravity.
John: If you draw a line through that point and cut along it both sides will weigh the same.

The teacher reflected on this, then asked how many agreed with John's statement. The majority of hands went up. Abandoning other plans, he suggested that they might test this idea out. He supplied the class with card and scissors and they set to work cutting out shapes, finding their centres of gravity, cutting through them and weighing the two parts. Looking at the pupils' work, you could see the majority chose regular shapes such as rectangles and circles, except for Ricky who cut out a circle with a long side arm. His results conflicted with those from the rest of the class. When asked how he had thought of a shape like that, he took a rectangle of card and balanced it on his finger, explaining:

> Look, the pieces can't weigh the same. This may be lighter (pointing to the apex of the triangle) but it goes out farther ... It's the moments, not the weights, that are the same. See here. This is balanced

now. Now if I turn up this side like this (Figure 19), I am not changing the weight and the card tips up. When I bend this up I am changing the *moment*, the weight's the same—just nearer to the balance point.

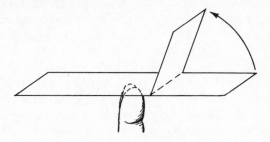

Figure 19

It is clear that Ricky has made the imaginative leap of perceiving the system in terms of the distribution of the weight. Having conceptualized it in this way, he is able to generate this clever little demonstration to prove it to himself. Those who were testing the idea empirically may have produced results which disproved the idea and yet have failed to understand the underlying reason. From the point of view of philosophy of science, it is interesting to note that it was the pupil who had made the conceptual 'leap' who was able to design the 'crucial' experiment.

It is often difficult for pupils to make distinctions between observations and interpretations of them. Learning that matter is composed of particles is considered as of equivalent status to the observation that metals expand on heating.

There are several ways in which the distinction can be made in teaching between observation and interpretation. One is to follow the suggestion of the SCIS programme and be explicit in introducing a theoretical notion that it is a scientific invention. Pupils are more likely to appreciate this, however, if on occasion alternative interpretations are also explored. The Nuffield science schemes have built-in opportunities for pupils to consider alternative explanations, for example the wave or particle nature of light. These opportunities tend to concern the big ideas in science and adequate appraisal of them requires pupils not only to understand the alternative theories in the first place, but to be familiar with a wide range of phenomena.

There are many less demanding situations when alternative interpretations can be explored, thus exemplifying the plural nature of scientific theory and distinguishing it from the world of sense data. The very existence of pupils' alternative frameworks means that within any class a range of alternative hypotheses may be generated. Accepting these and using them, as in the example of the balancing task discussed in this chapter, is a strategy for extending pupils' understanding of the process of theory-building and testing in science. Suggestions for opportunities to do this with the Nuffield science schemes have been outlined by Baddeley.[4]

The writers of the SCIS materials make a clear distinction between two kinds of inputs in the science classroom. First, there are experiences which extend pupils' knowledge of phenomena through observation, knowing that metals expand on heating, certain substances dissolve in water, green plants take in carbon dioxide in the presence of light. These, however, are distinguished from the inventions, which are introduced to interpret the observations made. Bearing in mind the discussion relating to philosophy of science in Chapter 1, making such a distinction in an explicit way in science teaching is important in that it reflects more clearly the nature of science itself.

Traditional science teaching used to emphasize a particular formula for pupils to use in writing accounts of experiments in which *method, results* and *conclusion* were separated. This approach has been criticized for a number of reasons. It is suggested that children learn through writing accounts in their own words, and formal structures inhibit this. The use of the term 'conclusion' can also be criticized as a relic of inductionism in that it suggests there is one unique interpretation of the data. However, encouraging pupils to make distinctions in their written work between observations made and interpretations offered is useful in reinforcing the distinction.

Opportunities can also be given for individuals or groups to explicitly generate alternative interpretations of an event, to invent their hypotheses. These can later be used as a basis for experimental design tasks to give pupils the empirical basis for selecting between the alternatives.

Turning from teaching an appreciation of the nature of the scientific enterprise to teaching a range of accepted scientific ideas, note the amount of new material that secondary school pupils are presented with in their courses: ideas such as force, energy, magnetic and electrical fields, electric current and potential difference, light and sound waves, atoms and molecules, charges and ions, genes and chromosomes. None of these can be perceived directly by the pupil. They are ideas or constructions imposed on experiences which make them make sense. But before they can be useful to pupils in this way, they have to construct the ideas in their imagination. Perhaps when we consider the number of new inventions which are introduced in secondary school science courses, it is not too surprising that many pupils find science difficult.

In the last two decades we have placed more emphasis on pupils' own activities in science lessons. We have placed faith in discovery; that by doing experiments pupils will better understand ideas. This may have a part to play, but experience alone is not enough. This approach will not succeed if the complementary role of imagination is not also recognized, and time given to encourage the development of this aspect of learning science.

It is common to see science lessons which end with the clearing up after the practical work is finished.[5] The time for the important discussion of how the experiences gained relate to the new ideas is missed. Activity by itself is not enough. It is the sense that is made of it that matters. Teaching strategies are needed which help pupils think and talk about the significance of their experiences and, most important, time for teachers to talk through pupils' experiences with them.

References

1. J. M. Atkin and R. Karplus, Discovery or invention?, *Sci. Teach.*, **29**, 45–51 (1962).
2. *SCIS Teacher's Handbook*, University of California Press (1974).

3. R. M. Jones, *Fantasy and Feeling in Education*, Penguin (1972).
4. J. Baddeley, Teaching and philosophy of science through Nuffield schemes, *Sch. Sci. Rev.*, **62**, 154—9 (1980).
5. M. K. Sands, Group work in science: myth and reality, *Sch. Sci. Rev.*, **62**, 765—9 (1981).

6

LEARNING SCIENCE
AND THEORIES OF
COGNITIVE DEVELOPMENT

In Chapter 1 of this book I presented the view that scientific theories are not deduced from data but are constructions of the human intellect.

An important proponent of this view is the epistemologist, Jean Piaget. Piaget and his collaborators in Geneva have made a major contribution to our understanding of children's thinking. Their work is based on a view that children's knowledge of a progressively more objective kind is constructed through interaction with the environment.

This chapter outlines the major features of the Piagetian position. However, it is not intended to be a complete review of Piaget's work for teachers. Readers interested in such reviews will find them elsewhere.[1,2] This section is included because of Piaget's contribution to a constructivist view of knowledge.

Currently there are some criticisms of the Piagetian position. These are outlined at the end of the chapter, together with a discussion of alternative models of learning.

Piaget worked as a biologist early in his life and he relates his ideas about learning to those concerning biological adaptation. He suggests that as children learn more about their environment they become better adapted to it. This process of adaptation Piaget has called *equilibration*. This takes place when a person assimilates an experience and in doing so adjusts or accommodates his knowledge structure to it.

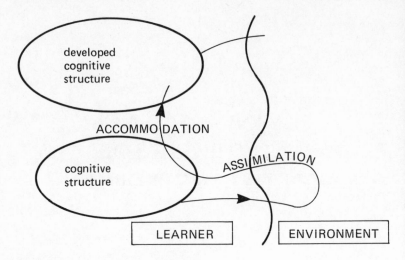

developed
cognitive
structure

ACCOMMODATION

cognitive
structure

ASSIMILATION

LEARNER

ENVIRONMENT

Figure 20

In Chapter 3 an example was given of two girls experimenting with the force required to pull a cart. They pulled a cart with a spring balance along the horizontal and saw that the spring balance appeared to read zero. This they recorded: it was information assimilated. However, it was clear from their comments that they did not understand how this could happen. Their expectations were different. They could not adjust their framework of thinking to accommodate the information. In Piagetian terms, equilibration has not taken place. To Piaget learning is essentially an active process in which the learner constructs his knowledge through interaction with the environment and the resolution of the cognitive conflict which may occur between expectations and observations. In fact, it is the need to resolve the cognitive dissonance that provides the intrinsic motivation for learning.

As children's experiences get more extensive the structures they develop become more encompassing. Figure 20 represents aspects of this developmental process in which information from the environment is assimilated by the learner. It interacts with the cognitive structure already present and as a result that structure is changed; accommodation has taken place, resulting in a more developed structure. What is assimilated depends not only on the environment, but on the learner's existing cognitive structure. If the dissonance is too great, assimilation will not take place at all. If there is no dissonance between an experience and a learner's cognitive structure then the information is assimilated without a change in the structure taking place at all. This suggests that for effective learning the principle of *moderate novelty* needs to be applied. Some of the records of pupils' classroom observations described in Chapter 2 are an illustration of this.

Through these processes of disequilibrium and subsequent equilibration new intellectual structures are developed which incorporate the preceding structures and consequently development is through an invariant sequence of hierarchically ordered stages. So, for Piaget, although maturation and various social and physical experiences are necessary for development, the essential dynamic process is that of equilibration.

Such a view of learning as equilibration or adaptation between the learner and the environment places the learner in an active role. The child is seen as the architect of its own knowledge.

One of the developmental features described by Piaget is the progression from egocentric to more objective thought. Young children start to make sense of events through their own bodily sensations. They tend to see the world with themselves as an agent. Young children have difficulty in imagining events from a perspective which differs from their own. They find it hard, for example, to imagine how a particular view of a landscape would appear to a person in a position which is different from their own. They also tend to explain events in terms of their action on a system, rather than in terms of the properties of the system itself. A class of 12-year-olds were making some observations about an experiment on floating and sinking. They were shown two beakers each containing a clear liquid, and an egg was lowered into each one. In one beaker the egg floated, in the other it sank. The pupils were asked to suggest possible reasons for the difference. In the majority of cases, the reasons were given in terms of the difference in the properties of the eggs or the liquids. However, one pupil suggested it was because one egg was put into the beaker more gently than the other. In this case, the explanation is in terms of his action on the system, rather than the properties of the system itself. Egocentrism is evident in various aspects of children's thinking about natural phenomena. Science teachers will recognize the problem that arises in teaching elementary ideas about light rays or paths. There is a tendency in some pupils to mark arrows on light 'rays' going from the eye to the object. In doing this, pupils take themselves as the starting point and consider the line of sight rather than the path of the light. To do the latter involves decentring from the position of 'viewer' and considering the system from an external frame of reference.

A further example of such egocentricism arises in pupils' understanding of a vacuum as an active agent. 'The vacuum sucks up the water like me sucking milk through a straw.' It is difficult for many 11- and 12-year olds to dissociate themselves from the phenomenon, and to interpret it in terms of the imbalance between the internal and external air pressure.

So far I have outlined general features of Piaget's developmental theory. However, the main contribution of Piaget's work has not been his general description of the mechanism for development of children's structures of thought. It is the extensive and detailed investigations which he and his collaborators have undertaken to describe the specific characteristics of children's thinking at different ages.

The cognitive structures which are central to Piaget's theory are of a logical or mathematical nature. They describe the form of a child's thought as opposed to its content. These structures Piaget suggests develop in stages. Two of the stages concern themselves with schoolchildren, the stage of concrete operations which develops from the age of about 5 to age 12, and the stage of formal operations, which develops during adolescence.

Concrete operations are identified as those performed directly on objects. The objects may be concrete or they may be symbolic, such as numbers or statements. Reversibility of thought is an important characteristic of this stage. A child appreciates that certain operations on a system can be reversed. A row of ten stones can be spread out and returned to their original positions, and hence their number is seen as an invariant property. A deformed ball of plasticine can be remoulded to its original size. Understanding this, the child can appreciate that such quantities as number, volume and weight are conserved under certain transformations.

The child is also able to classify objects into classes in a range of ways, including hierarchically organized classes. He can put objects into order using a range of variables such as length or weight. He can also use simple inferential logic to solve problems of the following kind.

If water in beaker A is hotter than water in beaker B, and water in beaker B is hotter than water in beaker C, which beaker has the coldest water in it?

The limitation of the thinking of a child at this stage, however, is his inability to think hypothetically. In experimenting he does not consciously set up a proposition to test and control the necessary variables in testing it. As a result, his solutions are achieved through trial and error.

The basic characteristic of formal thinking, which develops during adolescence, is the ability to manipulate propositions. A clear example is the use of hypothetico-deductive thinking, where the pupil sets out a range of possibilities and tests reality against them. Pupils at this stage can consider combinations of variables, appreciate the need to control certain variables in experimentation, and can separate relevant from irrelevant factors in their testing procedures.

A further characteristic of this stage of thinking is the setting up of mathematical models, specifically involving the concepts of ratio and proportion. This has implications for pupils' understanding of a range of scientific laws and concepts which are based on linear proportion: not until pupils are at the formal stage will they understand and operate at higher than an intuitive level with ideas such as speed, density or the law of moments.

Piaget's results suggested that children begin to develop formal thought by about 12 years of age. However, surveys undertaken in England by Shayer[3] and in America by Lawson and Renner[4] show that the majority of children do not develop formal operations until much later in the secondary school. This, it is argued, has implications for the science curriculum in secondary schools if what is taught is to be within the grasp of most pupils.

Currently, there is some controversy as to the validity and utility of the so-called stage theory. It is recognized that the ability of a pupil to use a certain logical operation, for example proportional thinking, depends on his familiarity with the context within which a task is set. Pupils may control variables competently in one task but not in another. This means that it is pupils' behaviours and responses which can be labelled as fitting a specific stage, not necessarily the pupils themselves. This context effect on performance calls into question the usefulness of applying a 'matching model' to prescribe the teaching materials which are appropriate to the learner's stage of development.

Such a matching model, described in some detail by Shayer and Adey,[5] has three components:

(1) the level of cognitive demand of a topic in the curriculum is analysed, and the topic is allocated to a level in the Piagetian stage taxonomy;

(2) pupils are tested in order to determine their level of cognitive development;

(3) the curriculum is planned so as to match the level of demand to the level of development of the learner.

This approach can give some guidance in the general planning of science courses over the years 5–16. However, there are problems in applying it to particular classes or to individual children. Some problems are organizational and raise questions of how instruction can be successfully individualized to match the requirements of all pupils in a class. Other more fundamental problems have been discussed elsewhere[6] and will be only briefly commented on here.

First, there is the question of adequately analysing the level of demand of a topic in the curriculum. The level of demand of a topic can depend on the way it is taught. For example, a teacher's guide may recommend that a particular topic is treated in a way that demands hypothetico-deductive thought with pupils generating hypotheses and testing them experimentally. The topic could, however, be treated in a way that did not make these demands and meaningful learning could still take place.

The second problem with the model lies in the assumption about the coherence of the concept of a 'stage'. If a pupil as a result of being tested is allocated to a particular stage, what is the probability of him performing at this level in another context? Studies vary in the answers they give to this question. The more carefully conducted studies indicate a reasonably high degree of association between levels of performance on one task and that on another.[7,8] However, the question arises as to whether this is adequate to make educational predictions at the individual level.

The third issue concerns a question of priorities in the curriculum. There is evidence to suggest that particular operations can be taught in the context of teaching a science topic. The necessary proportionality operations can be taught in the context of calculations on the mole, the law of moments can be used by pupils who are not assessed as operating at the formal level. Such pupils may not be able to generalize the use of proportional reasoning to other topics, but as science educators we might consider it an important end in itself that these particular scientific principles are understood.

In this debate about the validity of the stage theory it is not the results of Piaget's investigations which are being questioned, it is the interpretation being placed on them which is under review.

Currently there are three interpretations, each with a significantly different implication for the planning of science courses. First, there is the structuralist position which suggests that each stage is characterized by the development in the individual of a set of structures which determine the operations that a person can perform. In addition, developmental factors are the main determinants of the rate of appearance of these structures. In this way of thinking, the operations a child can perform, and hence his capacity for learning, are age-dependent. The educational implication of this position is to adopt a 'readiness' model: wait until a necessary stage is reached before teaching a topic.

Another position for which there is some evidence[9,10] is that the operations pupils can perform are age-related but the limiting factor is the capacity of working memory—the amount of information a person can keep in mind at any one time.

A third interpretation rejects the idea that there is an age restriction on learning. Instead, it is suggested that the age and sequence in which tasks are successfully performed are simply a function of the complexity of the tasks and the prior experience of the individual.

This position has been argued by Novak,[11] who concludes that the data from a number of studies

. . . support a model of cognitive development that is not 'stage' dependent, but rather dependent on the framework of specific concepts and integrations between these concepts acquired during the lifespan of the individual.

Novak suggests that Ausubel's theory of meaningful learning offers science educators a more useful and valid model of learning than the Piagetian stage model. Ausubel, like Piaget, assumes that each individual organizes and structures his own knowledge. Where the Piagetian model focuses on content independent logical structures or operations, Ausubel postulates that knowledge is structured as a framework of specific concepts. He emphasizes the role of verbal learning and distinguishes between rote learning and meaningful learning, where new knowledge is related by the learner to relevant existing concepts in that learner's cognitive structure. Following from this, Ausubel suggests,

The most important single factor influencing learning is what the learner already knows. Ascertain this and teach him accordingly.[12]

As indicated here, Piaget's theory focuses on logical operations a pupil can perform, whereas Ausubel's theory concerns the structuring of content. It is important not to see these as mutually exclusive. In designing teaching material one needs to consider both the component ideas that are being taught and the way those ideas relate to one another. For example, in teaching the concept of density, one would need to consider children's prior experience of the component ideas of mass and volume and relate the teaching to these. But there is also the issue of the way these two component ideas are related in a formal (as opposed to an intuitive) understanding of density requiring proportional reasoning.

Many substantive concepts in the sciences take their meanings not simply through the network of other substantive concepts to which they relate, but through the nature or structure of the relationship between them. Content and structure should be complementary considerations in curriculum design.

There is one very important distinction, however, between these two complementary considerations. If learning new ideas depends primarily on what ideas a child already has, then it should be possible with a suitably designed sequence of instruction to teach any idea to a child at any age.

If, however, there are structures of thought which only develop with age and experience, then it could be inappropriate to give instruction in those ideas at too young an age.

Up to now the results of Piaget's experiments are our best indication as to the ages at which such structures of thought develop. However, as is indicated in the next chapter, pupils' previous experiences and familiarity with the context of a presented problem will affect the logical forms of thought they use to solve it.

References

1. H. Ginsburg and S. Opper, *Piaget's Theory of Intellectual Development: An Introduction*, Prentice-Hall (1969).
2. K. Lovell, *The Growth of Basic Mathematical and Scientific Concepts in Children*, ULP (1961).
3. M. Shayer, D. E. Kuchemann and H. Wylam, The distribution of Piagetian stages of thinking in British middle and secondary school children, *Brit. J. Educ. Psychol.*, **46**, 164–73 (1976).
4. A. Lawson and J. Renner, Relationships of science subject matter and developmental levels of learners, *J. Res. Sci. Teach.*, **15**, 465–78 (1978).
5. M. Shayer and P. Adey, *Towards a Science of Science Teaching*, Heinemann (1981).
6. G. Brown and C. Desforges, *Piaget's Theory: A Psychological Critique*, Routledge (1979).
7. M. Shayer, Has Piaget's construct of formal operational thinking any utility?, *Brit. J. Educ. Psychol.*, **49**, 265–76 (1979).
8. A. Lawson, R. Karplus and H. Adi, The acquisition of propositional logic and formal operational schemata during the secondary school years, *J. Res. Sci. Teach.*, **15**, 465–78 (1978).

9. P. Bryant, *Perception and Understanding in Young Children*, Methuen (1974).

10. R. Case, Intellectual development from birth to adulthood: a neo-Piagetian interpretation, *in* R. S. Siegler (ed.), *Children's Thinking: What Develops?*, Wiley (1978).

11. J. Novak, An alternative to Piagetian psychology for science and mathematics education, *Stud. Sci. Educ.*, 5, 1—30 (1978).

12. D. P. Ausubel, *Educational Psychology: A Cognitive View*, Holt, Rinehart (1968).

7

LOGIC AND INTUITION
IN CHILDREN'S THINKING

In his writings about children's thinking Piaget makes a distinction between two kinds of knowledge; knowledge based
on physical experience and what he calls logico-mathematical
or operational knowledge.

Recently, a great deal of emphasis has been placed on
the consideration of pupils' logical capabilities or level of
operational thought in planning science activities.[1] It is argued
that much of the orientation of modern science courses
which place the pupil in the position of the scientist require
the abilities which Piaget associates with *formal operational
thought*; hypothetico-deductive reasoning, the ability to raise
and test hypotheses, to see the need to control variables in
making inferences from data and to impose quantitative
models on observations, specifically that of proportionality.

Formal thought is a way of manipulating propositions;
a way of processing ideas. What the pupil learns and under-
stands as a result of experience depends not simply on the
manipulation of ideas, but on the nature of the ideas themselves; that is, on the conceptual schemes the pupil brings to
the experience.

In his book *Identité et réalité*, Emile Meyerson[2] made
the distinction between causality and legality (which Piaget
later developed in his first work on children's causal thinking[3]), describing two processes by which inferences or predictions are made about phenomena. In causal thinking,

predictions or explanations are based on the individual's conceptual scheme, arguments are built in previous experience.
Legality refers to the individual's recognition of the logical
necessity of certain predictions; it is argument based on the
form of statements with no reference to their content or
meaning.

This section shows how the two modes of thinking are
inter-related. First, it is argued that causal thought is prior to
operational thought in determining pupils' activities and
understanding. Second, examples are given to show how
adolescent pupils confuse causality and legality in making
inferences. Last, evidence will be presented to show that,
when it comes to pupils' acceptance of ideas and their understanding of them, it is their causal thinking on which they
rely.

Some of the excerpts used in this chapter are discussed
at greater length in a paper which is included in the Appendix.
The paper describes the semiquantitative aspect of pupils'
thinking in science and outlines a method for representing it.

Carl and Richard are in the middle of an activity studying friction between different surfaces. They have pulled a
block of wood across different surfaces, using a spring
balance, and have noted the reading in each case.

Richard: We pulled it on the wood floor, a note-
book, a bristly rug, a soft board and a
tile floor.

Carl: Let's put it on the glass.

The boys repeat their measurement on a
large, glass-covered table.

Carl: 200 grammes! It's smooth, I thought it
would be less.

Carl continues pulling the block along
the glass to the edge.

Carl: 175 grammes.
Richard: Where?
Carl: Seems odd. When you put it on the glass,
as soon as you get near the edge, it takes
less force to pull it, while you pull it in
the middle it's pretty even. At the end it
jumps down.

This observation by Carl obviously surprises both of the boys, as they expected a constant reading on the balance. Repeating the observation showed the same result. Not satisfied to leave the issue unresolved, the boys then suggest several hypotheses and test them out until they are satisfied that they have found an explanation. Richard suggests: 'Maybe we are not pulling it evenly.' Implicit in this statement is the thought that the friction will depend on the speed at which the block is pulled. Richard attempts to control this factor by using a battery-driven vehicle to pull the block at what he assumes to be a constant speed. Another trial was made.

Carl: Did it change? (Referring to the spring balance reading.)

Richard: Yes, but it got continually lower. I think that may be inertia though.

Having controlled one possible variable, Richard now raises another hypothesis, that the change in the reading is due to inertia. (Later, he explained that his idea here was that it takes more effort to get something going than to keep it going, and this might have been the cause of the fall in the spring balance reading.) To test out this idea he turns the tractor round, starting it off from the edge of the table.

Richard: When it goes this way, force decreases. The other way it increases.

Carl: Maybe it's not level. Force would lessen going down, as gravity is helping you.

Richard: It looks level, though.

Having rejected the inertia hypothesis, Carl then suggests a further idea: that the change in reading is due to a sloping surface. Richard is dubious because the table appears level. However, the issue is finally resolved when the boys use a spirit level and find the table does, in fact, slope down at the edges. The issue is resolved, the question answered. The boys have interpreted what was originally a surprising observation in terms of an explanation they accept: that of the incline.

Certainly, this sequence shows the boys' ability to use hypothetico-deductive thought, and to select experimental situations which would test those hypotheses. However, without causal frameworks concerning inertia or the effect of the

slope, would the hypotheses have been raised at all? Also, if it had not been for the original surprise in the uneven spring balance reading arising from an expectation that it should be constant, there would have been no investigation in the first place.

In a similar experiment, Cathy and Jane also draw on their causal frameworks in suggesting what needs to be controlled.

Jane pulls the wooden block along the floor with a spring balance and notices an increase in the reading as she pulls. She does it again.

> Jane: It's more.

> Then, noticing that in pulling it she was increasing the angle of the spring balance with the floor, she adds: We had better keep the thing parallel . . . the force finder parallel with the floor.

Repeating the measurement now gives a constant reading.

In the examples discussed so far, the pupils have the necessary understanding of factors involved in the experiments, the necessary causal frameworks, to resolve an issue in question to their own satisfaction. Of course, this does not always happen. The following sequence of behaviour concerns a pupil, Stephen, testing out his hypothesis using a well-designed experiment, yet not being able to reconcile his observations with his ideas.

The apparatus Stephen was observing had been set up to demonstrate the linear expansion of a metal rod on heating, and was similar to the apparatus shown in Figure 18. Stephen starts by heating the bar with a bunsen burner as he is told and observes that the bar glows red. He removes the burner and observes and records its change in colour again. Repeating the experiment, he notices the straw jerking. He goes on heating and the straw moves slightly to the right, returning back again slowly when the burner is removed. He puzzles over this for a short while and examines the needle and straw. He then replaces the needle with a wooden matchstick and repeats the experiment. The straw again rotates. When he was asked what he was testing out, Stephen explained:

The heat makes the straw move. It pushes it away from it. This (indicating the needle) is metal and will conduct heat, so I am changing it for a wooden matchstick which is a poor conductor—but the straw still moves. I don't know why.

Stephen's idea about heat as a kind of motive force emanating from the burner and being transmitted to the straw suggested the experiment he tried. When the observation did not support this idea, he was at a loss to interpret the results. Despite having the necessary thinking skills in raising and testing a hypothesis, his conceptualization of what was happening was not leading him to make sense of his observations.

Pupils' conceptualizations of events are important, therefore, in suggesting fruitful experiments, in enabling them to suggest hypotheses which can be tested out and in governing the factors they consider important to control in their experiments.

Conceptual frameworks can also hinder experimentation. In some instances, they may be so well formulated and firmly held by pupils that, instead of acting as a source of ideas to test, they restrict empirical observations. The following sequence shows this occurring.

Jane has been experimenting with a simple pendulum to find out what she can do to make its period shorter. She has tried changing the weight of the bob, carefully controlling the position from where she releases it, and tapping the table each time the pendulum swings back to her. She then shortens the string and repeats her observations. Lastly, she releases the bob, first with a small, then with a larger initial amplitude. The whole sequence of activities indicates Jane's awareness of the need to vary one aspect at a time in order to make inferences. When she was asked what she would do to make a pendulum with the shortest period, her reply was:

Jane: I'd bring it all the way up . . . (pause) and give it a hard push.
Teacher: The push makes a differences, does it?
Jane: Yes.
Teacher: How can you tell?
Jane: Well I know that. I have just done it before . . . like a ball if you hit it harder it goes faster.

Here we see in the case of the variable 'the initial push', instead of appealing to the results of her experiment (legality), Jane relies on her previous experience, her causal framework, in predicting that pushing the pendulum will shorten the period. However, she goes on to demonstrate her idea to the teacher.

> Jane: So ... (she gives the bob a push and it swings right over its supporting bar) like if you push it, it goes all the way round, but if you let go it goes like that. (Lets go without pushing.) Oh ... I had it mixed up. Wait.

Jane gives the pendulum a slight push and taps the table, then repeats just letting the pendulum go.

If you push it, it has to go farther.

If it had not been for the teacher's intervention here, Jane would not have tested the effect of the push on the period of the pendulum, but would have relied on previous experience in making her inference. Instead she realized that the faster initial speed was compensated for by the greater distance travelled in a swing; she accommodated the unexpected result (that the push made no difference to the period) into her previous framework.

Jane had accommodated her expectation, her causal framework, to the results of her controlled experiment. Legality and causality had been reconciled.

Pupils' confusion of causality and legality

Tim, an 11-year-old, was doing some introductory experiments with springs. The teacher had introduced the activity by letting the pupils wind their own springs on tubing of varying thickness, using differing gauges of wire. Tim had wound a selection of springs of different wire on various tubes. He had hung weights on each of them, then removed the weights to see if they returned to their original length.

Talking to the teacher at the end of the lesson, he commented:

> Well, we were working with aluminium wrapped on a fat tube and aluminium wrapped on a skinny tube and thin copper on both and fat copper on both. A skinny tube seems to ... everything is wrapped tighter. It does not pull out as much after the weight is off. We had an aluminium on the skinny tube which did not change at all after the weight was off it got wrapped so tight.

Here, Tim is not only reporting his conclusion from a controlled experiment: 'that springs wrapped on a skinny tube do not pull out as much as springs wrapped on a fat tube'—he is introducing an explanation—'everything is wrapped tighter'. The inference arrived at empirically is justified to Tim, not only by the logical necessity of the way the experiment was conducted and the results inferred. He had to make the results 'make sense' to himself by introducing an explanatory device or causal thinking.

One of the difficulties with younger adolescent pupils is to help them distinguish between these two aspects: the empirical data and the explanation. When pupils are asked to plan an experiment it is quite common for them to tell you, instead, what the results will be and why. One 13-year-old boy was asked to plan an experiment about a pendulum. He was shown two pendulums which took different times to make one swing and was told that this could be due to their having different lengths, different weights or both. He had to describe the experiments he would do to find out which was correct. He wrote:

> You could do an experiment because the weight is smaller because the smaller one swings the fastest because the other one picks up more weight as it swings, but the string does not make no difference at all.

Obviously, doing an empirical test involves suspending judgement. If a pupil thinks he knows the answer already, the test must appear superfluous.

Knowledge and belief

Pupils need to be able to 'make sense' of results in terms of having a causal explanation, not simply the results of an empirical test. This is shown clearly when the two seem to conflict.

When Jane and Cathy were making their own springs, Jane hung weights on the springs, measuring both their extended length and their diameter. In her report she writes:

> The springs did not return wholly to its original length. But yet the diameter did not change. Why?

Possibly she was thinking of extending the spring like rolling out a piece of clay, increased length being compensated for by decreased diameter. The matter was obviously not resolved for her.

Richard investigated the extension of his springs under increasing loads. The graph he plotted (Figure 21) was far from linear.

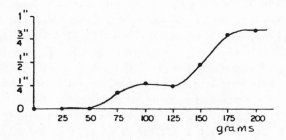

Figure 21

Richard's comments show his reservations about his observations:

> A spring stretches in spurts. I don't believe this but my graphs point to it.

In order not to believe the results, Richard must have had some expectations, some sense of what the data would show, which led him to question and later repeat his findings.

Legality or the form of an argument itself is not enough. Intellectual satisfaction comes from having constructed an adequate interpretive framework.

In the history of science there are many examples where scientists' beliefs rather than their empirical results have been seen to govern the progress of their enquiries. In the latter part of the eighteenth century there were conflicting views about the nature of heat, and specifically whether bodies change in weight on heating. In a paper, 'An Inquiry Concerning the Weight Ascribed to Heat', Count Rumford describes a series of experiments he undertook to find an answer to this question. He indicated that initial inquiries had convinced him that a body acquires no additional weight upon being heated. He then describes an experiment in which flasks containing equal weights of water and alcohol were weighed in a warm then a cold place. He reports his surprise at finding the flask containing the frozen water weighing more than the other. The experiment was repeated and the sceptical scientist even checked the accuracy of his balance at different temperatures. Following this result, he reluctantly comments, 'I could not conceive of any other cause for the augmentation of the apparent weight of water upon freezing than the loss of so large a proportion of its latent heat as that liquid is known to evolve when it freezes.' The matter did not rest there, however. After developing his measurement techniques further, he repeated the experiment, this time making sure that the vessels were at the same temperatures when their weights were compared. This time no change in weight was recorded. Rumford suggested that his earlier result was due to 'the vertical (convection) currents which they produced in the atmosphere upon being heated or cooled in it, or to unequal quantities of moisture attached to the surfaces of the bottles, or to both these causes operating together'. He thus concludes: '. . . it may be presumed that we shall never be able to contrive an experiment by which we can render the weight of heat sensible'.

The persistence shown in this sequence of experiments is notable: one might speculate whether Rumford would have continued with this line of inquiry if his initial expectation had been different. The sequence also illustrates the complex network of ideas which Rumford was operating with when devising his experiments and interpreting the

results; ideas about buoyancy, convection currents, condens-
ation, as well as the factors possibly influencing the accuracy
of his measuring instrument, his balance. It is the scientist's
awareness of these factors and the way they impinge on one
another that govern the design of the investigation and the
controls used.

By comparison some tasks used by children as exercises
in experimental design, in psychology experiments or in
school science lessons appear very sterile and contrived.
There tends to be an artificial structure imposed on tasks
with specific variables to be investigated and others to be
controlled, without reference to the conceptual framework
which gives rise to these particular variables being isolated
and considered for inspection. In reviewing the procedures
children actually go through in solving these problems, it is
not surprising that they embed their arguments in a causal
framework, as several of the examples in this chapter illustrate.

I am not arguing here that the form or structure of
pupils' thought is unimportant. What is important to realize,
however, is that the form of an argument is not the only
aspect to be considered. The context within which a problem
is set, the familiarity of the ideas to the pupil, will all affect
the logical structures the pupil will bring to the task.

The effect of context on pupils' perceptions of problems
and their ability to solve them is indicated in a series of
experiments by Donaldson.[4] She comes to the conclusion
that:

> Whan a child interprets what we say to him his
> interpretation is influenced by at least three things
> —his knowledge of the language, his assessment of
> what we intend (as indicated by our non-linguistic
> behaviour), and the manner in which he would
> represent the physical situation to himself if we
> were not there at all.[5]

Wason and Johnson-Laird conducted a series of experiments to study rational thought in adults.

> Our concern is simply this: given a set of assertions,
> to what extent can the individual appreciate all
> that follows from them by virtue of logic alone,

and remain unseduced by plausible, but fallacious, conclusions?[6]

The results of their studies indicate that the content of problems is important. If the causal and the logical requirements of tasks conflict, then subjects tend to base their arguments on the causal aspects rather than on logical reasoning.

> For some considerable time we cherished the illusion that . . . only the structural characteristics of the problem mattered. Only gradually did we realize that there was no existing formal calculus which correctly modelled our subjects' inferences, and second that no purely formal calculus would succeed. Content is crucial, and this suggests that any general theory of human reasoning must include an important semantic component.'[7]

The relationship between logical reasoning and causal thinking on science tasks has been studied by Linn.[8] She has investigated the influence of expectations on pupils' logical reasoning about experiments. Pupils were presented with an experimental situation and were first asked to list the variables they thought were involved. They were then told what the relevant variables were. In the experiments the pupils then conducted it was found that they were more likely to control those variables which they had initially identified as relevant. Linn concludes:

> Our research suggests that accurate knowledge of the variables and recognition of the variables that are important has an impact on the likelihood of efficient use of educated guesses. So, one aspect of any procedure to improve the likelihood of logical reasoning being employed in these situations will be to provide useful information about the variables.

Children's conceptual understanding appears to be the crucial determinant of their experimental behaviour. The case for science education has been made by some as a vehicle for developing rational thought. Curriculum materials have been developed with this as an aim.[9] It appears from the studies described here that if a person's logic suggests an outcome which is in conflict with expectation it is the latter which takes priority.

It might be argued, therefore, that it is people's intuitions in science which need educating rather than their capacity for logical thought.

References

1. M. Shayer, Conceptual demands of the Nuffield 'O' level physics course, *Sch. Sci. Rev.*, 54, 26—34 (1972), M. Shayer, D. E. Kuchemann and H. Wylam, The distribution of Piagetian stages of thinking in British middle and secondary school children, *Brit. J. Educ. Psychol.*, 46, 164—73 (1976).

2. E. Meyerson, *Identité et réalité*, Alcan.

3. J. Piaget, *The Child's Conception of Physical Causality*, Routledge (1930).

4. M. Donaldson, *Children's Minds*, Fontana/Collins (1978).

5. Ibid., p. 69.

6. P. C. Wason and P. N. Johnson-Laird, *Psychology of Reasoning*, Batsford (1972).

7. Ibid., pp. 244—5.

8. M. C. Linn, When do adolescents reason?, *Eur. J. Sci. Educ.*, 2, 429—40 (1980).

9. See, for example, the aims of the Science Curriculum Improvement Study, *SCIS Teacher's Handbook*, University of California (1974).

8

FROM THEORY TO PRACTICE

Whenever we plan and teach a science course we make decisions, whether explicitly or implicitly, about the aims of the course. For example, is it to be a course that is appropriate for all secondary school pupils or is it to be a preparation for pupils specializing in science? Is the course to be responsive to the interests and ideas of young people or is it primarily to reflect the structure of the discipline? What image of science does it promote—is it science as a body of knowledge or is there a place for inquiry and speculation on the part of pupils?

The 1981 policy statement of the Association for Science Education[1] lists six aims for education through science which might be summarized as follows:

(1) understanding scientific concepts,
(2) the development of cognitive and psycho-motor skills,
(3) the ability to undertake inquiries,
(4) understanding the nature of the scientific enterprise,
(5) understanding the relationship between science and society,
(6) the development of a sense of personal worth.

The document indicates that all young people at some point in their schooling should have experiences which lead to the achievement of all these six aims, although it recognizes that the needs of different young people may demand different emphases at various times in their schooling.

Developing and teaching courses which reflect this

balance is a very real challenge, not least because of some possible inherent conflicts between the aims themselves. This book has explored some of the issues involved in producing a satisfactory synthesis between just two of the aims: the acquisition of knowledge and the use of pupils' own inquiries in the pursuit of further knowledge. The tension between these two components has existed for as long as science has had a place in the school curriculum.

Over the last 100 years documents on the role of science in general education have reflected this tension. In a report, *Natural Science in Education*, published in 1918,[2] the authors make an eloquent claim for science in the school curriculum in terms of the general faculties it develops:

> It can arouse and satisfy the element of wonder in our natures. As an intellectual exercise it disciplines our powers of mind. Its utility and applicability are obvious. It quickens and cultivates directly the faculty of observation. It teaches the learner to reason from facts which come under his own notice. By it, the power of rapid and accurate generalization is strengthened, without it, there is a real danger of the mental habit of method and arrangement never being acquired.

In 1936 the Science Masters' Association published a report, *The Teaching of General Science*,[3] in which it states three main contributions that science makes to general education:

(1) utilitarian or vocational: it helps the pupils in their everyday life, or may be necessary in their future occupations;
(2) disciplinarian: it teaches them to think; it sharpens their minds;
(3) cultural: its inclusion is desirable because it forms an essential part of our social heritage.

Again, the claim is made that science makes an important contribution to the development of pupils' general faculties, although the report later adds a cautionary note:

... we would point out, however, that *experimental* evidence has shown quite definitely that the possibilities of transfer of training are much smaller than had formerly been supposed.

The 'process' aims of science education have also been of concern to American curriculum developers since the 1950s.[4] The curriculum development projects in secondary science which have taken place since the 1950s in Britain and America have attempted to foster the skills of scientific inquiry and to promote an understanding of scientific principles and their application to everyday life.

As I indicated earlier, the traditional synthesis between these two aims has tended to promote an inductivist view of science based on the premise that all scientific knowledge derives from sensory experiences. This perspective has been reinforced over the years by views about child-centred education, as articulated by such people as Froebel, Dewey and Piaget.

Incidentally, it would be incorrect to suggest that psychologists and philosophers of science have been influential in shaping the science in our schools. Rather the community of science educators has invoked such theoretical 'support' as is necessary to give credibility to 'common sense' views about the nature of science and of children's learning. The problems that exist both with the inductivist view of the nature of science and with the 'accretion' view of children's learning have been outlined in earlier chapters. It appears that it is necessary to piece together a new synthesis between content and process in science education which brings together both a different philosophy of science and a new perspective on learning. This involves the recognition that the science that children learn beyond primary school is more than natural history; it goes beyond the exploration and classification of aspects of the environment. Pupils are being introduced to theoretical ideas and conventions of the scientific community, ideas which derive from the imagination and which may in time be superseded.

If this constructivist view of the nature of science is to be taken seriously then it has certain implications for secondary school science courses. This chapter gives a personal view of a number of these implications.

A developmental approach to science teaching and learning

Throughout the book, evidence has been presented which indicates that children use a range of intuitive ideas to make sense of their experiences. Some of these ideas, or alternative frameworks, are characteristic of the thinking of many children, and may persist despite instruction. Perhaps it is not surprising to note the similarity between some of the ideas of children and theories that have been important in the history of science itself (for example the caloric theory of heat or Aristotelean views of motion). Daily experiences of phenomena make some interpretations or models more obvious than others. However, it is very easy to view the notions put forward by pupils as naive and simplistic, and to pass them by, perhaps with disinterest. It is perhaps worth bearing in mind that some of these notions were given serious consideration in the scientific community in the past. By referring to the ideas and investigations of past scientists, some of the powerful ideas of young people can be explored in a way that treats them with respect. It has been suggested that, instead of ignoring the alternative frameworks that children have developed, science teaching programmes could benefit by taking greater account of them. By making their theories more explicit in the formal learning situation children are able to explore their implications and make comparisons between one 'framework' or 'theory' and another. They can also be given experiences which serve to develop their ideas or, if necessary, to challenge them. Various science teaching materials have attempted to do this. One of the most well-developed examples is the treatment given to dynamics by the Harvard Project Physics materials,[5] where the Aristotelean view is explored at some length.

Educators have always recognized the need to 'start where the child is'. Ausubel emphasizes this in the distinction he makes between 'meaningful' and 'rote' learning. In practice this is usually interpreted in terms of relating science teaching to experiences which are familiar to children in their daily lives.

However, perhaps in addition, teaching needs to relate to what is familiar to children, not just at the level of the world of events and experiences but also in their world of ideas. If children are encouraged to make their theories more explicit, these can be open for inspection and testing in the classroom. Children's own ideas in fact can provide the necessary raw material to exemplify the plural nature of scientific theory, and act as a starting point for pupils to design critical tests to distinguish between different interpretations.

Underlying this recognition that children's ideas as well as their experiences need to be taken into account in planning courses is a view of the learning process as taking place by conceptual change. The task for educators is to give pupils the experiences which encourage such change to take place. In preparing secondary science courses little attention has as yet been paid to what is known about the development of pupils' thinking. Such projects as Science 5/13 and the Australian Science Education Project have based their sequencing of materials on a Piagetian stage model. In this kind of scheme, ideas which involve the structures of formal operational thought such as arguing hypothetico-deductively, controlling variables or using proportional reasoning are not introduced until the adolescent years.

Shayer and Adey[6] report their analysis of the cognitive demand of a range of secondary science courses in terms of Piagetian levels, and the results of a survey of the levels of thinking of British schoolchildren. The findings indicate a mismatch exists between the logical demands of the science courses analysed and the level of thinking of most secondary school pupils.

Such an analysis may give general guidance on matching the demands of a course to the logical capabilities of the pupils taking it. It can be helpful in giving a general indication of the way ideas can be sequenced for teaching and at what age they might be introduced. However, there is more involved in taking account of children's thinking than simply paying attention to its logical component. In a previous chapter doubt was expressed about the Piagetian matching model and it was indicated that the content as well as the logical structure of a task affects pupils' performance.

In some science topics investigations of pupils' ideas indicate that these develop with age through a clear sequence, and a knowledge of this can be helpful both in deciding at what age to teach a topic and how to organize appropriate experiences for pupils: experiences which will aid their con-

ceptual understanding of that topic. Some of the interesting
approaches being tried which are based on this view of learning as conceptual change have been reviewed in earlier
chapters. Techniques which are being incorporated into these
approaches include providing opportunities for pupils to
make their own ideas explicit, encouraging the generation
and testing by pupils of alternative interpretations of phenomena, and giving pupils experiences which challenge their
current ideas.

The question of structure in the science curriculum

Such a view of learning through conceptual change has implications for the general organization of the science curriculum.
In his influential book, *The Process of Education*, Jerome
Bruner drew attention to the importance of the structure of
the subject to be taught:

> ... the curriculum of a subject should be deter-
> mined by the most fundamental understanding
> that can be achieved of the underlying principles
> that give structure to that subject. Teaching specific
> topics or skills without making clear their context
> in the broader fundamental structure of a field of
> knowledge is uneconomical in several deep senses.[7]

Much of the science curriculum development that has
taken place over the last two decades on both sides of the
Atlantic has indicated this concern for structure. The content
of science courses has been updated and their structure
changed to reflect recent developments in the conceptual
structure of the discipline. Paradoxically, this has been
coupled with a shift in pedagogy towards a greater amount of
practical work; practical work which in most cases is introduced to be illustrative or provide confirmatory evidence for
the presented theories. We tend to think that this 'practical'
approach makes the subject more 'relevant' and easier for
pupils to understand. Yet there is a sense in which the
approach is making even more intellectual demands on pupils
in that it requires pupils to relate experiences obtained in the
laboratory to the theoretical models being presented. The
pupils themselves, with or without guidance, need to make

the connection between the phenomena and the theoretical constructs: for example, to link the movement of levels of liquids in tubes to the increased motion of invisible particles which 'compose' the liquid, to relate the change in colour of a solution in a test tube to the concentration of hydrogen ions present. It is important to recognize that in science lessons pupils are involved in learning at two levels at once: they are exposed both to new phenomena and also to their accepted theoretical interpretation. Simply because teaching based on conceptual schemes is problematic does not mean it should not be attempted. However, the demands it makes on pupils need to be recognized. If pupils are unable to link the experiences given in the laboratory to the conceptual themes in the course, then the coherence that is apparent to the curriculum writer or teacher may not be obvious to the pupils, who may remember it simply as a series of disjointed experiences. Incidentally, the current debate over teaching science as separate disciplines or as an integrated course may be an irrelevant issue to many pupils who remember their experiences as a sequence of lessons, whatever the subject is called on the timetable. The key question is 'what is integrated by the learner?'

Even though they have difficulty relating the phenomena to the presented theory, some pupils are prepared to suspend judgement, to learn the rules or laws even though they cannot relate them to their experiences. They are able to maintain interest in the belief that at a later date what they are learning will make sense. On the other hand, many secondary school pupils, perhaps the majority, expect more immediate intellectual satisfaction. They are not prepared to wait weeks or even years before theoretical ideas presented in school can be related to their own experiences. Many of these pupils will never continue with their formal science education after leaving school. Such pupils need to be able to 'make sense' of the scientific ideas presented to them in a more immediate way.

School science may be remembered, but recalled as isolated experiences; some activity with glass blocks and pins may be remembered in much the same way as a snatch of a Wordsworth poem or an unrelated fact in history. It has not become part of the young adult's way of understanding the natural world. Unless the theory or formalism presented to pupils is learned in a meaningful way, it is soon forgotten as useful knowledge and not drawn on in the future: pupils revert to their intuitions or earlier frameworks. The problems that this can cause have been illustrated in earlier chapters. Designing a curriculum around major conceptual schemes may mean that most pupils finish their formal education in science neither understanding the theory they have been introduced to nor seeing the illustrative phenomena as particularly relevant or interesting.

If the orientation of science in general education is to help pupils develop a theoretical understanding which enables them to interpret and make sense of everyday experiences, to make pupils more 'at home' in the natural and man-made world they inhabit, then this may mean reassessing the science curriculum at two levels. It means selecting illustrative phenomena not simply because of the support they give to a theoretical idea, but because they are of practical use and everyday interest in their own right. It also means bringing the theoretical ideas within the compass of pupils' understanding.

In many areas of science, phenomena can be interpreted at a range of levels of sophistication, all of which are in some sense useful. For example, in the early years of secondary school, we expect pupils to understand current electricity in terms analogous to fluid flow in pipes. This model is quite effective in enabling us to predict or explain a range of everyday phenomena involving electrical circuitry; in this sense the model is 'right', it is adequate for its purpose. However, older pupils are introduced to a more sophisticated model in which electric current in wires is construed as a drift of charged particles through a lattice structure. This model is only 'better' than the previous one in that it accounts for a greater range of phenomena. A similar shift in the level of theoretical sophistication is encountered in several other topics, for example, in chemical bonding, the wave properties of light, inheritance and the molecular—kinetic theory of heat.

For pupils who have difficulty in understanding the theoretical ideas in science perhaps it is necessary to reconsider the level of theory presented. For example, are we justified in placing so much emphasis in basic science courses on the kinetic—molecular model when pupils have such difficulty in understanding it well enough to be confident in using it? Would it be more appropriate to accept a caloric notion of heat from younger secondary school pupils? After all, members of the building trade, for example, operate effectively in their calculations of heat conductivity of materials in terms of 'quantities of heat' and 'rates of flow'. From the pupils' point of view it is perhaps preferable to have a workable model to interpret phenomena, even if it has to be changed at a later date, rather than to be exposed to more sophisticated ideas which only confuse.

There are those who will oppose such a suggestion, arguing that we should never teach anything that has to be 'unlearned' later. In response, I would argue that such a view simply does not reflect much of our experience, either in formal learning contexts or in everyday situations. We are continually being placed in situations where we have to revise, develop or discard ideas in the light of new evidence. The challenge this faces us with in science education is to present theories to pupils so that they can be understood and yet not be taken as immutable truths. There is an important distinction to be made here between understanding and belief: it is possible and important to be able to *understand* alternative interpretations, those suggested by other pupils or other scientists, without necessarily *believing* any of them.

The 'experimental method' and science teaching

In appraising the role of practical work in secondary school science, a number of types of activity can be distinguished. There are those whose purpose is to extend pupils' knowledge of phenomena, others are used to illustrate and confirm 'accepted' principles. In addition, there is a case for including opportunities for pupils to undertake their own investigations, not in order to establish an important principle, but to gain some experience in planning an experiment using their own initiative. The focus of such activities is not the result obtained, but the steps along the way: the design of experiment, the choice and use of the apparatus, the careful recording and interpretation of the results. In order that children can undertake such investigations in as honest and thorough way as possible, time may have to be set aside from what is often the main orientation of the teaching programme.

These experimental exercises offer an opportunity to encourage individual initiative and imagination. They may be important in giving pupils experience of the rational—empirical approach to problem-solving. However, the skills they encourage, skills of careful observation, measurement and logical argument, are as relevant to the garage mechanic, electrician or dressmaker as they are to the scientist. The case for including exercises of this kind in science lessons is not to exemplify the way that science itself proceeds, but to encourage general rational thought, and to give pupils a sense of confidence in their own capabilities.

To illustrate the way science itself proceeds, the focus needs to be on competing conceptual systems. In a paper, 'Towards an integration of content and method in the science curriculum', Noretta Koertge states the following conclusion:

> To understand the growth of science and to get a balanced picture of both its fallibility and its claims to soundness, one must use a pluralistic approach and study at least two competing systems in detail.[8]

In reaching that conclusion, it is argued that science proceeds not by an inductivist approach of making generalizations about data, but that progress is made when an accepted theory competes with a new theory for the interpretation of data. Such a pursuit is very different from what has been characterized as the 'scientific method'.

Koertge proposes that case studies of competing theories from the history of science would be appropriate material for teaching the methodology of science. However, one need not search the literature on the history of science for examples of competing systems: pluralism in conceptual systems already exists among pupils in science classrooms.

Alternative frameworks suggested by pupils offer teachers readily available opportunities to illustrate characteristics of the scientific pursuit through the appraisal of competing interpretations or conceptions of events. Nor are new science teaching schemes necessary: as Baddeley[9] outlines, there are many opportunities within the current Nuffield science schemes to exemplify and test out competing theories which derive either from children's ideas or from the history of science.

A question of time

Science is not just natural history, and education in science involves more than simply extending the range of children's sense experiences (though it may also do this). It is about introducing children to the conventional scientific interpretations of events and helping them reorganize their ideas accordingly. Children need more than practical experiences for this reorganization in their thinking to take place. And yet, particularly in lower secondary school, it is the practical work, especially group practical work, which often occupies the greatest proportion of teaching time. Laboratory work is an important feature of science teaching, yet we may not be making the most of this important resource. In their survey of secondary schools,[10] the HMI report that

> (Science teachers) believed that pupils should have first-hand practical experience in laboratories in order to acquire skills in handling apparatus, to measure constants and to illustrate concepts and principles. Unfortunately, practical work often did not go further than this and few opportunities were provided for pupils to conduct challenging experimental invesigations.

They suggest that an important reason for this is the constraint imposed by examination syllabuses.

Not only do pupils need time to undertake practical activities, but more time is needed to make the most of those that are undertaken. Where activities are intended to illustrate some concept or principle, then time is required for pupils to consider their results and generalize the findings to new situations.

In a study on group work in science, Sands[11] reports that a major omission in lessons was the necessary 'follow-up' relating to the group work. Many such practical lessons end abruptly when the prescribed task is complete and little, if any, time is given to the interpretation of the results obtained, although this is just as important as the activity itself. Pupils need time to think around and consolidate the new ideas presented to them. After all, they may have developed their own ideas as a result of many years of experience. It is unlikely that they will easily adopt new ways of thinking as a result of one or two science lessons. As was suggested in an earlier chapter, opportunities to apply new concepts or ideas in a range of situations are important in consolidating pupils' understanding and helping to build a bridge between the presented theory and experience. Here there may be teaching techniques which can be borrowed from other school subjects. Just as science teachers have developed the necessary skills to organize group practical exercises, perhaps the time has come to consider the development of strategies to help children make more sense of those practical experiences. What is being suggested is not a return to a more didactic teaching, but an extension of the range of types of activities undertaken in science classes.

The suggestions made so far have one requirement in common, and that is *time*. It takes time to allow for speculative discussion in class, even more time is required if pupils are to follow up competing ideas or to undertake their own investigations. If the necessary time is to be allowed, then it appears inevitable that a careful appraisal of the content coverage of syllabuses is necessary. Of course, some hard decisions may have to be made as to which topics to include and which to leave out. But perhaps curtailing the syllabus is not too great a price to pay if as a result pupils gain greater confidence in their understanding of the ideas covered, and in addition have some time which can be specifically devoted to inquiries of their own, however simple.

The ideas suggested in this chapter indicate ways in which teachers can help pupils not simply to extend their sensory experiences through science lessons, but to understand the conventional theories and formalisms of the scientific community and to relate these to their experiences in a meaningful way. They suggest a role for teachers as mediators between the pupils' experiences and understandings and that of the scientific community.

The writers of the Bullock Report remind us of what this may involve in the following passage:

> What the teacher has in mind may be the desirable destination of a thinking process, but a learner needs to trace the steps from the familiar to the new, from the fact or idea he possesses to that which he is to acquire. In other words, the learner has to make a journey in thought for himself.[12]

References

1. ASE policy statement, *Education Through Science* (1981).
2. Report of the Committee on the Position of Natural Science in the Educational System of Great Britain, in *Natural Science in Education*, HMSO (1918).
3. Science Masters' Association, *The Teaching of General Science*, Murray (1936).
4. NSJA: National Science Teachers' Association Curriculum Committee, *Theory into Action* (1974).
5. *Harvard Project Physics*, Holt, Rinehart (1970).
6. M. Shayer and P. Adey, *Towards a Science of Science Teaching*, Heinemann (1981).
7. J. Bruner, *The Process of Education*, Harvard (1960).
8. N. Koertge, Towards an integration of content and method in the science curriculum, *Curriculum Theory Network*, **4**, 26—44 (1970).
9. J. Baddeley, Teaching the philosophy of science through Nuffield Schemes, *Sch. Sci. Rev.*, **62**, 154—9 (1980).
10. DES, *Aspects of Secondary Education in England*, HMSO (1979).
11. M. K. Sands, Group work in science: myth and reality, *Sch. Sci. Rev.*, **62**, 765—9 (1981).
12. The Bullock Report, *A Language for Life*, HMSO, 141—2 (1975).

APPENDIX

THE REPRESENTATION OF SEMIQUANTITATIVE THINKING IN ADOLESCENT SCIENCE STUDENTS

(Part of a paper given at the Seminar, 'Observation in the Science Classroom', University of Paris, March 1978)

The empiricists' view of science suggests that scientific ideas and theories are reached by a process of induction. Investigators, whether pupils or practising scientists, should proceed through a hierarchically organized sequence of processes, starting with observation of 'facts'. From such 'facts' generalizations can be made and hypotheses or theories induced. However, current philosophy of science suggests there is a fallacy here, namely, that hypotheses or theories are not related in any deductive way with the so-called 'objective' data, but are constructions, products of the human imagination. Their link with the concrete world comes about through the process of testing and possible refutation. In this way of thinking, observations take on a different significance. We can no longer consider them to be wholly objective, but influenced by the theoretical framework of the observer, whether it is that of the scientist or a pupil.

Because any theory is not related in a deductive and hence unique way to observations, there can be multiple 'explanations' of events. Pupils can and do bring alternate frameworks to explain observations which are in keeping with their experience and in this respect are not 'wrong'.

However, we may recognize them as partial and limited in their scope.

In summary then, 'alternate frameworks' exist through pupils' attempts to make sense of aspects of their experience for themselves. In that their frameworks do assimilate that experience they are not wrong, perhaps just not as inclusive as the accepted 'scientific' view. As with 'accepted theories', they derive partly from the imagination of pupils and are more than descriptions of events. They also influence and focus pupils' observations of future events, and may significantly affect what pupils may learn from organized science lessons.

It was with this perspective in mind that I undertook my study, which involved, first, identifying common alternative frameworks in pupils around age 11, and, second, following the pupils through a sequence of instruction to see to what extent and under what conditions these ideas changed.

The setting of the study

The work was carried out at the University of Illinois Laboratory School, in a general science class of 11-year-olds. The class was taught by a young male teacher whose mode of working was rather special. He organized the class into groups of 'research teams'. The pupils were encouraged to find their own answers to questions posed. At the end of a sequence of practical work on a topic, the pupils were expected to present papers to the class and debate their findings and the inferences they could draw from them. The teacher consciously tried to play down his role as an authority on science, emphasizing his function as facilitator, organizer and chairman of discussions. The pupils were observed during three sections of work: 'balancing systems', 'stretching springs' and 'forces and motion'. The class met for an hour each day. The period of study extended over 3 months' work.

Four pupils were selected for detailed observation during this time: two boys and two girls. All the pupils in the class had been given five Piagetian formal level tasks and the four pupils selected spanned the stages from concrete to formal level thinking. During the teaching sequences these four pupils' activities were monitored by video tape and audio tape. They were also interviewed by the author before and after each unit to ascertain the extent to which their frameworks had been changed by the sequence of study. Tapes were selectively transcribed for later analysis.

The outline of the findings

For each of the three units of work there were four classes of protocols:

(1) Protocols of the ideas pupils had at the beginning of a unit, indicating misunderstandings or limited understanding.
(2) Protocols of group work with apparatus. These indicated the way pupils' frameworks influenced their activities. They also showed the extent to which their frameworks changed in the inferences they drew from their experiences.
(3) Protocols showing the pupils interacting with the teacher. These at times indicate the communication difficulty that exists between the pupils and the teacher because of their different frameworks.
(4) Transcriptions of class discussions at the end of each unit, which indicate the alternate interpretations pupils place on similar experiences.

The method of representation

Each of these classes of events I could have reported on and discussed descriptively. However, in order to illuminate my analysis of the protocols, and to highlight the complexities of the thinking they showed, I made an attempt at developing a method of representation. It should be clear that the method of representation is a descriptive one, not an analytic one. Its purpose is to expose more clearly the variety of features involved in the pupils' thinking about causal events. It is also a dynamic model: it represents changing features. In this respect it differs from, say, Piaget's attempt to model children's thought using formal logic, which gives an essentially static representation.

It also differs from Piaget's modelling in that it attempts to represent both the structural features of thought (for example, operations such as implication, reciprocity, negation) and the contextual aspects (the content upon which those features operate). This, I believe, is an important distinction, since there is growing evidence that the thought processes pupils use depend to a great extent on the context of the task and the familiarity of the child with it.

I shall outline the features in the system of representation using the protocols from the classes of events outlined earlier. In so doing, I hope to indicate something of the substantive findings of the study *and* the method of representation.

Features of semiquantitative thinking

Statements by pupils about the natural world often reflect the connections they perceive between aspects of events.

If you push this it will slide along.

Winding a spring tighter makes it stronger.

In both these examples the pupil has abstracted two aspects of a system and linked them. The first statement can be represented in a general way as in Figure 22. The system from which the abstractions are made is S. The aspects focused

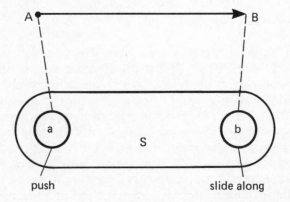

Figure 22

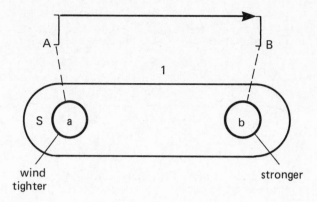

Figure 23

on are a and b. These are integrated into more general concepts (represented by A and B), which are linked as shown by the arrow.

The second of the statements is similar to the first, but indicates more internal structure in that the two concepts 'winding tighter' and 'stronger' imply magnitude, and the statement indicates the direction of the relationship between these quantities. This is represented in Figure 23. In this case the concepts 'winding tighter' and 'stronger' are represented by number lines and the relationship between them by a directed line or arrow. The fact that the arrow goes between the tops of the number lines indicates the direction of the relationship (increase in 'winding tighter' implies an increase in 'strength'). The converse would be represented as in Figure 24 (p.92).

The aspects of the system that pupils are paying attention to may not be given verbal descriptors by them. In this case, the observer labels those aspects. In some cases it is important to illustrate some confusions which exist for pupils in using words to describe what they are referring to. The same word may map on to different aspects of the system, or different words may refer to the same thing. To illustrate this, a linguistic domain is included in the representation.

The following example is a simple illustration of its use. An 11-year-old boy, Carl, is working on a simple balance, in which washers used as weights can be hung from four equally

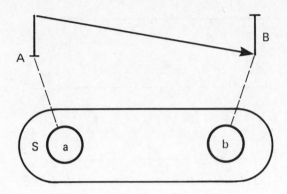

Figure 24

spaced hooks on each side of the pivot. Carl has set up the balance with two washers a distance of two hooks out on each side. He is asked what will happen if the right-hand washers are moved further out still. He replies

> It will go down . . . it is farther from the leverage point, it has more pull, it is heavier . . .

then

> These two (referring to the washers) are the same weight, but the closer you put them to the middle, the ones that are farthest will go down. I don't know why.

This is represented using the notation so far in Figure 25.

I will now consider a more extended excerpt: that of two boys, Tim and Richard, involved in an investigation on the strength of springs which they make for themselves by winding different wires on dowel.

> Without any discussion between them, the boys collected different types of wire, two objects to wind the wires on (¾ in dowel and ¼ in diameter glass rod) and a cup containing ball bearings. They take these to their lab table and start winding springs of different diameters using the various kinds of wire.

1   T.   Let's wind a copper wire on a thin tube and an aluminium wire on a wide tube and see what happens.

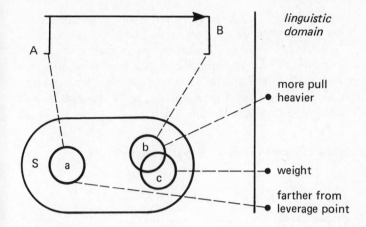

Figure 25

2 R. (Not paying attention to Tim, Richard hooks a spring on to a cup of ball bearings.) Now I'm going to test to see the effects on this spring under a weight.

3 T. What are you trying to prove now, Rich?

4 R. No. (Does not release the weight and puts down the spring.) Let's get a ruler and see how much it stretches. (The boys both go to get a yardstick.)

5 R. Aluminium is 3 in long (measuring unstretched length) and the copper is $2^1/_8$ in. (Hangs the cup from the aluminium spring.)

6 T. How far is that off the ground?

7 R. It doesn't matter.

8 T. Pull it up and see if the spring doesn't move any.

Richard is holding the spring with the cup suspended from it in one hand and has the yardstick held vertically in the other. In response to Tim he lifts the spring up slowly.

9 T. O.K.

Later Tim explains to E.:

10 T. This is farther up and gravity is pulling it down harder (Tim is holding two marbles, one higher than the other) . . . I mean the gravity force is still the same but it turns out it is pulling harder the farther

away. No, I had better rephrase that. The higher it
gets the more effect gravity is going to have on it
because ... um ... because like if you just stood
over here and someone dropped a pebble on him, it
wouldn't hurt him. But like if I dropped it from an
aeroplane it would be accelerating faster and faster
and when it hit someone on the head it would kill
him.

Richard's framework is shown in Figure 26.

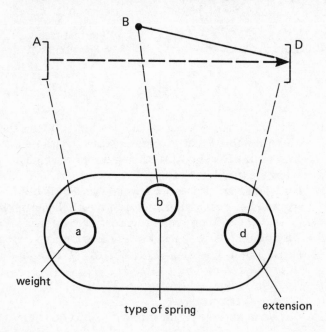

Figure 26

He identifies the weight applied as a factor he is looking
at, and then clearly focuses on the extension. He then measures
the extension for springs made of two types of wire. The
relationship between the type of spring and the extension is
the one Richard is focusing on, but, as a later sequence
shows, he knows the applied weight also has an effect.

Tim focuses initially on the type of wire and the thickness of the tubes they are wound on, clearly not controlling

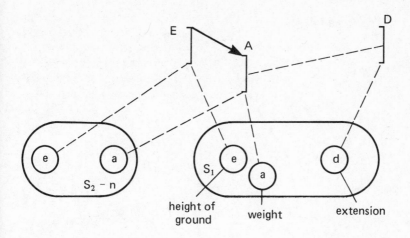

Figure 27

variables. He then interrupts Richard with the question 'How far is that off the ground?' (statement 6). This reveals an aspect of Tim's framework which is not present in Richard's (see Figure 27). Tim's previous experiences and thinking (S_{2-n}) lead him to suggest that the weight of the cup of ball bearings (concept A), and hence the extension of the spring, depends on its height off the ground (concept E).

He tests this out in this situation and finds the length of the spring does not change as he raises it. However, what effect this refutation has on his subsequent thinking about height and weight is not great as the later passage indicates (statement 10).

The representation of more complex frameworks

I have already discussed examples of pupils using semiquantitative relations between concepts. In some cases it is clear that pupils are assuming a particular mathematical form for the relationship, the most common one being that of linear proportionality. Where this occurs it is represented as in Figure 28. There are examples where pupils are aware of two concepts each mapping on to a third so as to compensate for each other. The representation is shown in Figure 29 (p.96).

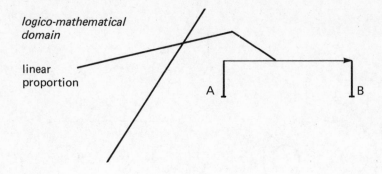

Figure 28

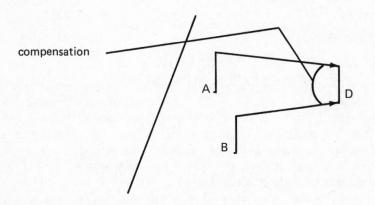

Figure 29

I will now consider two examples, both illustrating a form of compensation. The first is taken from an interview with Richard in which he is presented with a horizontal track along which he can project ball bearings of varying weight.

1   E. Can you see what this (plunger) does?
2   R. It makes the balls roll along here (the track).
3   E. How does it work?

Richard shoots a ball, then considers the distance the balls will go.

4   R. Well, this catch (plunger). If I set it at the first catch that would not give it as much force.

Richard then starts lifting the balls comparing their weights.

5 R. This one ought to go farther.
It wouldn't have as much friction, it's not being pulled down the most . . . it's mainly weight that is important.

6   Actually, the heavy balls might go farther because of their inertia. If they get started they are harder to stop . . . but I was thinking of weight increasing friction.

7   I guess it would be that it's too light to go far, there must be a certain point where weight increases friction before they even themselves up and then weight begins to weight it down more, so there must be a middle weight.

Richard shoots several balls.

8 R. There must be a middle weight (pointing to the ball that went the farthest). It won't have too much friction and won't get too little inertia.

The sequence reveals a complex framework (Figure 30, p.99). Richard indicates that the setting of the spring-loaded plunger (variable A) will affect the distance the balls will go (statement 4). He then turns his attention to the effect of the weight of the balls (variable D). Weight appears to affect the distance travelled in two ways: the lighter the balls the less the friction (variable E), and hence the further the balls will go (statement 5). On the other hand, Richard also argues that the heavier balls, once moving, will have more inertia and hence keep going (statement 6). He then considers the combined effect of these two influences. Rather than the two compensating for each other in a simple way, thus excluding weight as a variable, Richard's compensation idea here implies a nonlinear relationship so that a certain 'middle weight' goes the farthest.

This same idea about a 'middle weight' occurs when Richard investigates the factors affecting the period of a pendulum.

Richard places the golf ball on a long string and sets it swinging. While it is still swinging he winds up the string.

1   R. It's already beginning to do it . . . you have to shorten the string.

Richard turns to E as though he has finished.

2   E. (After a five second pause.) Is there anything else that might make a difference?

3   R. I'm not too sure, but I think there is another equal weight balance like there was over there.

4   There will be a middle weight where things will swing faster because when it gets too heavy the thing won't go vary far after it will be caught. If it's too light it won't gather enough speed coming down to go up very far.

From now on Richard is looking for the 'middle weight'. He hangs the polystyrene ball on one string and the rubber ball on the other and adjusts them to the same length, pulls them back carefully to the same amplitude and releases them.

5   R. This one (rubber ball) is actually covering the same distance as this (polystyrene) in a shorter time. This one (rubber) must be closer to the 'middle weight'.

Richard replaces the rubber ball with the small metal one and repeats the test. He continues testing the balls in pairs.

6   R. Maybe there is no middle. Somehow these seem fairly equal (in period of swing). One weighs more than the other, so I guess that would make the centre of weight (middle weight) somewhere in between.

Richard lines up the balls in order of their weights.

7   R. I think it is more likely that the centre of weight, of where it would go fastest, is some object right about there. (Points to a place in the line.)

8   E. Could you do an experiment which would show someone whether objects of different weights have different periods?

Richard selects the metal ball and the cork ball.

9   R. Same size.

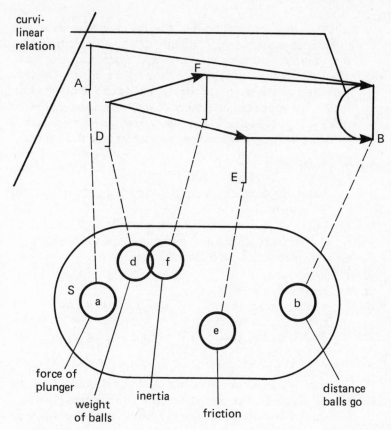

curvi-
linear
relation

Figure 30

10 E. Why is that important?
11 R. Well, that will prove whether size has any effect on
     it ... they are the same size, otherwise you could
     argue that since they weren't the same size that
     could be the reason.

The second example of compensation which I will
discuss here is taken from an interview with Jane on the
factors which influence the period of a simple pendulum.

Jane demonstrates an ability to control the variables
while experimenting. She first places a small metal ball
on the string, sets it swinging and accurately taps the

table when it returns to her. She removes the metal ball and hangs a tennis ball on the string, pulls it back the same amount as the metal ball and again taps the table when the ball returns to her. She then removes the tennis ball and winds up the string, hangs the tennis ball on again and repeats her observations. She then pulls the string down again and, still using the tennis ball, sets it swinging with first a small, then a larger initial amplitude.

1	E.	What can you tell?
2	J.	It goes a lot faster when it is higher.
3	E.	Then what would you do to make a pendulum with the shortest period?
4	J.	I'd take this one (small metal ball) and bring it all the way up . . . (pause) and give it a hard push.
5	E.	The push makes a difference, does it?
6	J.	Yes.
7	E.	How can you tell?
8	J.	Well, I know that. I have just done it before . . . like a ball if you hit it harder it goes faster so . . . (Jane demonstrates this on the equipment by pushing the pendulum.)
9		Like if you push it, it goes all the way round, but if you let go it goes like that (lets go without pushing).
10		Oh . . . I had it mixed up. Wait. (Jane gives the pendulum a push and taps the table, then repeats, just letting the pendulum go.)
11		If you push it, it has to go farther.

Jane's initial activity on the task clearly indicates her ability to control variables. She isolates the kind of bob, the amplitude and the length of the string for separate study. An interesting feature occurs when she is asked what she would do to make a pendulum with the shortest period (statement 3). In addition to suggesting shortening the string, she adds that she would give it a hard push (statement 4). In justifying this, it is interesting that she draws on previous experience, and perhaps did not feel that she needed to test this factor at all (a case of theory influencing observations). However, she does demonstrate what she means and is caused to reconsider her prediction.

Figure 31 represents only the latter part of this interview (statements 3—11). Initially, Jane is suggesting that a

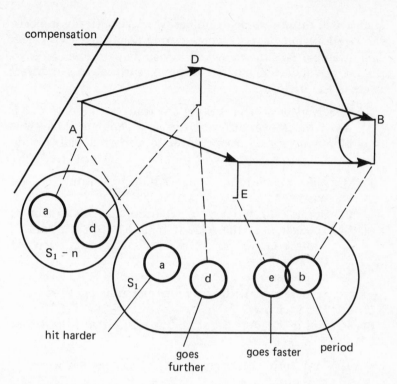

Figure 31

harder push makes the bob go faster, and by implication give a shorter period. However, when she demonstrates this she realizes another factor is involved—the harder she pushes, the further the bob will go, compensating for the greater speed.

Representation of change

There are many examples of discussion and activities during classroom work which show thinking becoming more elaborate as pupils become more involved in studying a system or problem. This reflects the comments of David Hawkins, who suggests the need for a 'messing about phase' in science inquiries before more structured investigations are undertaken.

We have already seen an example of a development of thinking in the case of Jane and the pendulum experiment.

Here I will outline some examples which specifically indicate the development of frameworks during practical activity. The first example occurs when two boys, Richard and Carl, are pulling a wooden block over different surfaces to see differences in the friction.

> The boys have been testing the force required to pull a wood block over different surfaces. They now take their block and spring balance over to a sheet of glass on the floor.

1   C.   200. It's smooth, though I thought it would be less.

2   R.   Where?

3   C.   Seems odd. When you put it on the glass as soon as you get near the edge it takes less force to pull it; while you pull it in the middle it's pretty even. At the end it jumps down.

4   R.   Maybe we are not pulling it evenly. (He leaves and comes back with a tractor and runs another trial.)

5   C.   Did it change?

6   R.   Yes it did, but it got continually lower. I think that may be inertia though.

> Richard turns the tractor around and makes a run in the other direction.

7   R.   When it goes this way force decreases. The other way it increases.

8   Maybe it's not level. Force would lessen going down as gravity is helping you.

9   R.   It looks level though.

> The boys borrow a spirit level and find that, in fact, the glass sheet is not completely horizontal.

When the sequence starts (Figure 32), the boys have a simple framework underlying their activity. It simply relates the roughness of the material they are testing to the spring balance reading (C). When they pull their block along a glass sheet, however, Carl notices the spring balance reading is not even—it changes at the edge of the glass (statement 3). Richard suggests a hypothesis—they are not pulling it evenly (statement 4). He attempts to remedy the situation by pulling the block with a toy motorized tractor. This is interesting in itself in that it suggests a strong connection for the

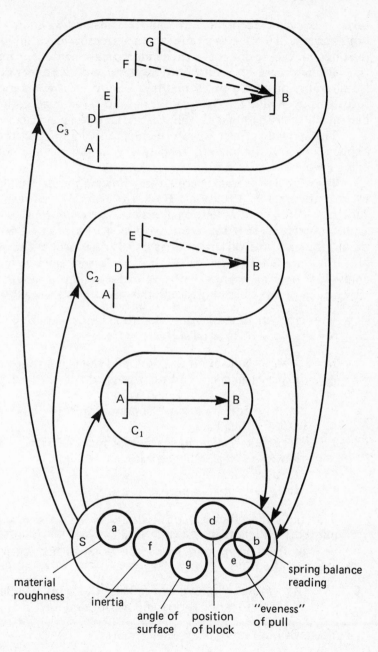

Figure 32

boys between a constant force and a constant speed. The boys run another trial, this time with the tractor, and still the reading on the spring balance changes (statement 6). This time Richard suggests a further hypothesis to do with inertia. (Is he implying that, once something is moving, it takes less force to pull it along?) The test he tries, however, suggests he had another idea in mind as well, that of an uneven surface.

The sequence finishes with the boys concluding that the explanation for the uneven reading lay in the surface not being level.

Two further examples are given, showing pupils 'tuning in' to experimental situations. Both are examples involving Jane and Cathy. In the first example, the girls are doing the same activity as the one described for Richard and Carl: pulling blocks over different surfaces. The sequences shows how they gradually consider a range of factors such as the angle of the spring balance with the surface and the speed at which they pull in obtaining results they trust (see Figure 33).

The girls are investigating the force required to pull objects along horizontal surfaces.

1   J.   Yes, let's do it on the floor and then let's sweep a place real good and then let's do it and see if there is any difference. O.K.?

2   C.   (Cathy nods.) It won't show up on this (looking at the spring balance).

3   J.   It might. If we had accurate ones I bet you it would . . . real, real accurate ones.

4   C.   Real, real little.

5   J.   Like half a gramme.

Jane pulls the block along the floor. As she does so, she allows the angle of the spring balance with the floor to change from being parallel to the floor to making an angle of about $30°$ to it.

6   J.   It's more! We had better keep the thing parallel . . . the force finder parallel with the floor.

The girls both note this in their report.

7   C.   O.K. . . . force finder . . . parallel—with—the—floor.

8   J.   What is the force?

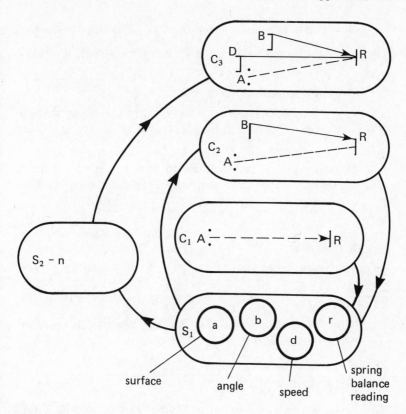

Figure 33

Jane pulls the block along the floor keeping the spring balance parallel with the floor.

9	J.	25
10	C.	25 what?
11	J.	These . . . see it went up to here.
12	C.	Kilo.
13	J.	Kilogrammes, no, grammes! Grammes, Cathy. G R stands for grammes.
16	J.	O.K. Let's do it on this table. (Feels the table surface with hand.) Shall we just call it fairly rough?
17	C.	Yea.
18	J.	Same brick and everything except for the surface.

Jane starts to pull it along the table and stops suddenly.

19 J.   But we should do it at the same speed, shouldn't we?

They return with a toy tractor.

20 J.   We had better do it over, Cathy, because we were probably not doing it at the same speed on the floor.

Jane hooks the tractor on to spring balance, runs it across the table watching the spring balance reading.

21 J.   About 25 to . . . 50, I mean. We'd better do it one more time.

Run it again.

22 J.   50, right?
23 C.   Yea.
24 J.   O.K.

The girls write down the data and repeat the measurement on the floor.

25 C.   25. It's less.

Mr. Guthrie approaches.

26 MG.   I see you are writing your results down. That's good.
27 J.   I always do. I can't remember them.
35 J.   Let's write down all the variables . . . We could get another block and do it on the same surface.
36 C.   No, let's do it on other surfaces first. Let's do it on the sandpaper.

They do so.

37 J.   (Looking at spring balance.) 125. Now let's get a different kind of block and do it exactly the same. No, let's put weights on our block first, Cathy.

In the second example the girls have substituted a cart on wheels for the wooden block and are experimenting to see the force required to move it, first on the level, then on an incline of varying slope. This sequence is illustrated in Figure 34.

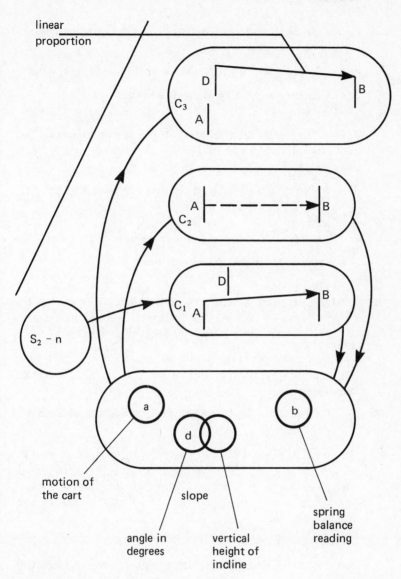

linear
proportion

D

B

C₃

A

A

C₂

B

D

B

C₁

A

S₂ – n

a

b

d

motion of
the cart

slope

angle in
degrees

vertical
height of
incline

spring
balance
reading

Figure 34

The next day the girls set up an inclined plane with a
wooden board on bricks and planned to pull a cart up
it using the tractor again and the spring balance to
measure the pull.

1   J.   We'll find how much force it takes just to pull it along flat first.

Jane attaches the spring balance and tractor to the cart.

2   J.   O.K. here goes. Read it as it comes to you.
3   C.   Oh. I can't.

Jane leans over and tries to read the spring balance. The cart has run off the plank by this time so she sets it back on again and starts it back the other way.

4   J.   Um . . . ZERO!! Gosh, it doesn't take anything to pull that . . . it says . . .
5   C.   Zero.
6   J.   Try it backwards and forwards again.

They repeat the reading several times.

7   C.   O.K., it's zero.
8   J.   O.K., zero at 0°. Let's clean this up, it's so messy it's pitiful (referring to the clutter of books, blocks and other things they had collected on their table).

The girls now proceed to perform the same experiment on an incline and realize they need something to measure the angle.

9   J.   We have to find something to measure the angle. Mr. Guthrie?

The girls indicate that they want something to measure angles in degrees. MG brings a protractor. They said they had used one before. Jane set the board on the bricks so that the angle was 10°. Cathy looks at the spring balance.

10   C.   About 75.

Jane looks at the protractor again and remeasures the angle to be 6°. She raises the incline to 10°.

11   C.   150—no, 125 grammes.

Jane looks at the spring balance.

12   J.   In between that and 125.
13   C.   It was 150. It should be. Try again.
14   J.   No. It was 125. No, this was 6, Cathy, double is 12.

That would be about—so see every 2 grammes would be a 25.

15 C. (Talking at the same time as Jane.) But look, you are doubling the degrees practically and 75 should come out. (Shouting) You are doubling the degrees!

16 J. We're not—we will now if you want to! (Adjusts angle) What is it now? (Checks angle is 12°) Ready?

17 C. About.

Jane sets the tractor to run up the plank again.

18 J. 150?

19 C. Yea. So if you have 12° it's 150.

20 J. So I would say from this every 2° is 25 grammes.

In this sequence we see that the girls expect a finite reading on the spring balance when pulling the cart along the horizontal. They are very surprised when they notice the reading is zero, and never understand why this should be. This is a very clear example of the gulf between observation and interpretation. As with the example of Tim's framework for height and weight mentioned earlier, the girls made an observation which they cannot assimilate into their present framework. However, the observation by itself does not suggest an alternate framework for interpreting the data. Jane is simply left 'not understanding' what she sees.

This takes me back to a point I made in the introduction to this paper, where I indicated the shortcomings of the rational empirical view for learning science. Here we have an example. Jane and Cathy had collected their data, they had repeated the measurement, even, to see it was reliable, yet they were not able to 'understand' it, to 'make sense' of it. They were not able by themselves to make the leap of imagination required to abandon an Aristotelian framework and adopt a Newtonian one. Here help was clearly required.

INDEX

n after page reference refers to note number.